CW00394481

Python Programming and SQL

A Comprehensive Guide for Beginners to Mastering Python and SQL

Hands-On Exercises and Step-By-Step Guidance to Get a Competitive Edge and Achieve Your Career Goals!

Philip Robbins

© Copyright 2023 - All rights reserved.

The content contained within this book may not be reproduced, duplicated or transmitted without direct written permission from the author or the publisher.

Under no circumstances will any blame or legal responsibility be held against the publisher, or author, for any damages, reparation, or monetary loss due to the information contained within this book. Either directly or indirectly.

Legal Notice:

This book is copyright protected. This book is only for personal use. You cannot amend, distribute, sell, use, quote or paraphrase any part, or the content within this book, without the consent of the author or publisher.

Disclaimer Notice:

Please note that the information contained within this document is for educational and entertainment purposes only. All effort has been executed to present accurate, up to date, and reliable, complete information. No warranties of any kind are declared or implied. Readers acknowledge that the author is not engaging in the rendering of legal, financial, medical or professional advice. The content within this book has been derived from various sources. Please consult a licensed professional before attempting any techniques outlined in this book.

By reading this document, the reader agrees that under no circumstances is the author responsible for any losses, direct or indirect, which are incurred as a result of the use of the information contained within this document, including, but not limited to, — errors, omissions, or inaccuracies.

Table of Contents

PART I

–

Python Programming

Introduction

Computers can be categorized as machines with no inherent intelligence, but they have drastically helped to advance our world in countless ways. With computers, our world runs much more efficiently and error-free—we tell them what to do, and they deliver flawless results. Computer programmers are the people who communicate with computers in what are called programming languages, and they have been doing so for many years. These programming languages vary based on their working systems, just as human language varies based on region.

One of these computer programming languages is called Python, and in the computer realm this is a quite popular (and easy to learn) high-level programming language. This book will teach you Python in an intuitive way. Even if you have no experience with any programming language, you will be able to grasp the basics of Python and put them to use.

What is Python?

Python is a high-level programming language that is popular within the programming community. It is simple, versatile, and contains an extensive library of third-party frameworks. It is also considered to be one of the most popular modern programming languages, being highly accessible for beginners. You can even use it to create software in your programming domain of choice.

Accredited universities such as Stanford teach Python to computer science graduates as an introductory language. Many online courses that explore programming basics also use Python as the default language. As you can see, it's very prevalent and therefore highly useful to learn. For these reasons, I am happy that you have chosen this book to help you learn Python quickly and intuitively.

Who Am I?

If you search the Internet, you are likely to find thousands of resources available for learning Python. And while this is great, it can also be overwhelming—therefore, many beginners can get frustrated because they do not have concise instructions with a clear walkthrough.

My name is Philip Robbins, and I am determined to offer a clear pathway for beginners to excel. I have more than twenty years of experience working in the field of software development using Python, and I am an expert Python programmer. My love for programming started a decade ago, when I avidly played video games. It all started with my enthusiasm to mod a Pokémon game that I was playing. My will to successfully change a small bit of code to feel accomplished sparked excitement to understand programming logic and variables at a young age. With some modding experience, I was able to understand how programs work and spent time experimenting with different programming languages.

Fast forward a few years, and I started creating small scripts that could automate workflow. However, I had still not chosen a particular programming language, and this made it challenging to be an actual software program developer. All of the programming languages I had tried, such as C and Pearl, were challenging to implement and almost made me quit programming due to massive frustration many times. Fortunately, during those turbulent times

I discovered Python in its initial stages. Python first began as a hobby project by one developer, so its initial form was not very clean. Once it gained in popularity, however, fellow developers began to notice the open-source project. This spurred them to add in their own contributions as well. Thus, they effectively modeled it into the efficient programming language it is today.

Within a few months of learning Python basics, I began implementing my own pre-existing code into Python. I was astounded by the code's portability as well as its lack of clutter. Once I learned how Python worked, there was no turning back. I began writing my software and publishing them using different stores. Even though my main job was to create web applications, I successfully created several other side projects in various domains with the help of Python.

Now that I am proficient in Python, I am interested in helping people who are struggling to learn this coding language. Even when I was first modding games in the beginning stages, I always had a passion for quickly assisting people in learning programming. I use layman's terms to explain complex topics, and this has helped many of my friends and colleagues understand them better. My passion for programming and teaching has compelled me to write this book in order to help beginners who are new to Python.

How Can This Book Help You?

Though Python programming looks easy to implement, in truth it is not. If you have a thorough understanding of the several foundational topics Python contains and how you can utilize them to solve problems, this is incredibly helpful. As such, this book provides you with the theoretical knowledge you need to know in order to understand the foundations and practicality of the programming language you are trying to use.

To get the most out of this book, we recommend cognitive learning techniques. These will enhance your experience with this material.

- Use cognitive memory techniques such as Memory Palace to keenly remember the data. However, there is a difference between simply mugging up the required information in your brain versus formally storing it when using f cognitive techniques.
- Use mind maps to map different concepts in order to quickly implement them in your projects. Mind maps are cognitive learning tools that use visual excellence via a short diagram to remember large amounts of data easily.
- Use the passive recall technique to quickly review all of the topics you have learned in this book. Passive recall can also help strengthen your programming foundations.
- Don't just use the code given in this book. Instead, reimplement your code using similar strategies. Using the simple copy-and-paste technique will not help you in creating your code.
- Use the Feynman technique to explain all of the basic programming concepts you have learned in this book to someone unaware of the subject. You have a strong knowledge of the core foundations if you can explain concepts in simple terms.

As a programming language, Python expects you to be as innovative as possible. Therefore, if you treat programming with Python like solving a puzzle, then you will intuitively discover ways to trick your brain into creating complex code logic for addressing real-world problems. This book helps you to become as effective as possible with Python programming.

Chapter 1: Introduction to Python

Python is a powerful programming language that is easy to learn, has a strong foundation, and can support multiparadigm workflows. As a result, it is an excellent starting point for beginners who want to delve into programming. Python's popularity stems primarily from its lack of clutter and boilerplate code.

For example, writing a simple snake game in C or C++ usually requires 300 lines of code. In contrast, with Python you can limit the number of lines of code to less than 200. This significant difference in terms of implementation contributed to Python becoming the most popular open-source language in the world. Python quickly became the waypoint for the open-source revolution, with so many enthusiastic programmers and developers writing thousands of libraries for various computer fields.

History of Python

Guido van Rossum, who created Python, made it as a side project over the Christmas break. Using what he learned working with the ABC programming language, he made an interpreted programming language that is easy to understand and use. He first used Python to impress hackers in an online community with his knowledge of how Unix works.

But after getting feedback from his fellow programmers, he worked on it for a few months to make it better. So, he made a programming language that was easy and quick to understand. Guido van Rossum has been called the "benevolent dictator" of the Python community because of what he has done for the Python project. Open-source developers can be given this high award.

Python has always been one of the 10 most popular programming languages, according to TIOBE rankings, ever since it came out. Python's simple way of solving problems has helped it beat other programming languages, like Pearl, and become one of the easier ones for beginners to learn.

Python is based on the idea that there is only one way to solve a problem, which is different from the idea behind programming languages like Pearl, which is that there are many ways to solve a problem. So, Python gave the programming community the discipline it needed and made software development grow by a factor of ten.

Look at the Python Applications below to see how important Python was to programmers around the world.

Applications of Python

Python made its mark in many areas of science and technology today.

1. Web Domain

Python has had most of its early effect as a programming language on web technology. While Java was the most popular thing on the web, Python wasn't as popular. Over time, Python has become popular among web developers thanks to third-party frameworks like Django and Tornado.

In the twenty years since then, Python has become one of the most popular scripting languages for websites, second only to JavaScript. Python is a programming language that is used by big companies like Google, Facebook, and Netflix. A well-known web framework called Django can also help programmers write backend code for a number of APIs.

Python is also popular for automating tasks, so it is often used to make bots like Pinflux.

2. Scientific Computing

Python is popular with scientists because it is free for anyone to use. Also, programs like Numpy and Scipy make it easier for computer scientists to do experiments with less code. Since Python is also better at mathematical calculations and software, Scientists have no choice but to use it these days.

3. Machine Learning and AI

AI and machine learning are now two technologies that can be used together to give more jobs to developers. There are a lot of third-party libraries for Python, like Tensorflow, that are all about implementing Machine Learning algorithms.

Python is also very good at adapting to technologies like Deep Learning and Natural Language Processing. This makes it one of the main candidates to become a better language for making AI-related technology.

4. Linux and the Management of Databases

As businesses around the world grow, there is a big need for developers who can manage databases and internal systems well. Develop engineers need to know enough about different operating systems, like Linux, and they also need to know enough about Python to automate other procedures that are needed to test how well methods work on an internal network.

5. Penetration Testing and Hacking

Python is also used by hackers with both good and bad intentions. For example, white-hat hackers use Python tools that are widely used to do penetration testing. On the other hand, hackers with bad intentions use Python scripting to make exploits that automatically steal sensitive information from their targets.

Python's ability to be used in almost any area of computer programming has led to the development of several other high-level programming languages, like Go, Groovy, and Swift. Python spread the idea that programming should be as simple as possible.

Different Versions of Python

When Python came out at the start of the 1990s, it wasn't as good as it is now. Rossum built the library without any help from anyone else, so it had a lot of bugs and mistakes. But because Python was so popular right away in the programming community, hundreds of independent developers helped Rossum make a much bigger project in the two years after the first version came out.

Python was also able to get a lot of smart people to check and change the code because it was open source. Because of this, the Python core programming team has put out two main versions, Python 2 and Python 3, for developers all over the world in the last 20 years.

In 2022, Python 2 is still used by a lot of programmers, even though Python core developers no longer support it. Choosing which version to use depends on what you are doing.

Python 2

Python 2 is now an old version that came out in the year 2000. Still, it has been the most used version of Python for more than 20 years. Python 2 is easier to use and has a lot more frameworks and libraries from outside sources that can be used for development.

Even though Python 2.7 will no longer get official updates after 2021, it is still the best version for many software domains. But it's hard to move all of the frameworks and libraries from Python 2 to Python 3, so many companies still use Python 2 as their default version.

Python 3

Python 3.9 is the most recent version of the programming language that developers can use. Python 3 is faster and gives developers many more classes for working with the core library. Compared to Python 2, it is also easy to keep up with.

Which one Should I Choose?

Which version of Python you use should depend on what kind of software you are making. For example, a lot of data scientists use Python 3, while developers who work with legacy software use Python 2 to connect components.

Note:

All of the Python code in this book is written in Python 3, since it makes more sense for beginners to start with a newer version.

Why You Should Learn Python

Python started to become more popular in the early 1990s, when companies all over the world started to use the internet's power to make complex web applications. Traditional programming languages like C and C+ were hard to learn and made it hard for programmers to write good code quickly. During this time, Python helped a number of companies make libraries that worked well with the C and C++ libraries they already had. Also, programmers started using Python to quickly deploy code because it was easier to work with than other high-level languages.

By learning about some of Python's many benefits, you can see how powerful and easy it can be for developers with different backgrounds in computer science.

It Is an Interpreted Language

Instead of using a compiler to run instructions like other programming languages do, Python uses a new piece of software called an interpreter. Instead of taking a lot of time to run a program with a compiler, the interpreter uses modern computer techniques to parse the code before the program is run. This dynamic parse time can cut down on the time you have to wait while the program is running. Python also uses parts of natural language to get rid of unproductive ways of coding that can slow down production. Because of how it is set up, it is also easy to automate programming in Python, which is why system developers and Linux administrators like it so much.

It is Open Source

One of the first things that led to the open-source revolution was Python. Because Python is open source, you can change any code and share it on your own. Open-source culture also makes it easier for programmers all over the world to share their knowledge and resources to make libraries and frameworks that can help developers make new projects.

As a beginner, having one-click access to both complex and simple projects can help you understand how programming works and make it easy to make new, creative projects.

It Supports Multiple Paradigms

To write and run code, different programming languages use different programming paradigms. Java, on the other hand, uses an object-oriented paradigm, while C uses a functional paradigm. A programming paradigm changes how developers work and how they try to solve a problem.

Python supports multiple paradigms, like the structured, functional, and object-oriented paradigms. This makes it a good choice for programmers who want to solve problems in different ways.

It Uses a Garbage Collection Mechanism

Managing memory is an important skill for application developers to have. High-level languages such as Java and C use complex data management techniques. Even though these mechanisms work perfectly, it takes a lot of time to keep them in good shape. In Python, on the other hand, memory is handled by garbage collectors. You can easily use the data and variables that this strategy no longer uses.

It Is Easy to Understand

One of the many reasons developers like Python is that it is easy to read. All of the code is easy to understand, which makes it easy to keep up. When Python code is easier to read, its quality goes up, and when the quality goes up, it takes less time to fix bugs in the code.

Portability

Python can also run on any operating system, which makes it easy for developers to use in different ways with just a few hours of work. Users only need to install the interpreter on their system for Python programs to work.

For instance, let's say a programmer writes a program for Linux that makes it easy to automate SQL database management. Then, anyone who has access to the code can place it on Windows or Mac machines by changing a few parts of it.

It Has Great Custom Libraries

If you want a programming language to be widely used, it needs to have great libraries. Developers can play around with a lot of these libraries in Python.

Aside from these custom libraries, programmers can also make interesting software with the standard libraries that the Python core development team gives them.

It Supports Component Integration

Python makes it easy for programmers to add new code to code that has already been written. Also, its advanced integration of components makes it a good choice for making advanced customization options for different software applications.

Component integration keeps developers busy by adding new features to older software so it can run on newer operating systems.

It Has a Great Community

The Python community is extremely helpful and can help new programmers quickly solve any problems they run into while writing code. Aside from Python forums, resources and well-written guides from a variety of experienced programmers can help developers get past any problems.

Since there are a lot of open-source Python projects on GitHub, a hobbyist programmer can just look at the code to see how complex logic is implemented in software.

How to Install Python

To write Python code, you must install an interpreter on your system. Without this interpreter, no developer would be able to write or run Python programs. Python can be put on any modern operating system because it can be moved around. In this section, we'll talk about how to install Python on Linux, Mac, and Windows.

How do I Install Python in Linux?

Since most programmers use Linux as their main operating system, we'll start by installing Python on your local machine using Linux. Linux is a free operating system that most programmers and businesses use. Because of this, Python is already on many Linux distributions.

To see if Python is installed on your Linux system, use the CTRL+ALT+N command to open a new command terminal.

When the new command terminal opens, type the following command into it.

Terminal Code:

```
$ Python3
```

If Python is installed on your system, the license information for the version of Python that is installed will show up in your terminal.

If you get the output "command not found," on the other hand, it means that Python is not installed on your system. Since Python is not installed, you can now use the package managers for Linux to install Python for different distros.

Before installing any software on Linux, you must first update all the tools on Linux and make sure there are no conflict errors that could stop Python installation.

Terminal Code:

```
$ sudo apt-get upgrade
```

You can use the code above to update package files on a Linux system that is based on Debian.

Use the following Pacman command to upgrade packages on an Arch-based system.

Terminal Code:

```
$ sudo pacman -S
```

After upgrading the packages, you can use the commands below to install Python on your Linux system.

Terminal code for Debian systems:

```
$ sudo apt-get install Python3
```

Terminal code for Arch systems:

```
$ pacman -u Python3
```

Look at the official Python documentation to install in other Linux distributions like Gentoo and kali.

How do I Install Python on macOS?

macOS is the operating system that Apple makes by default. Python 2 is often installed as native software because it is built with UNIX support.

Make sure you open a new terminal from Settings > Utilities > Terminal to see if macOS is installed on your Apple-supported hardware.

Enter the following command once a new terminal has been opened.

Terminal Code:

```
$ python3
```

If you don't see a Python version message, it means that Python is not installed on your system. To install Python from scratch, use homebrew.

Terminal Code:

```
$ brew install Python3
```

How do I Install Python on Windows?

Windows is the most used operating system in the world, based on the number of people who use it. Many people and programmers use Windows because it is easy to use, and there are many ways for Python programmers to quickly get their code into Windows.

To install Python on your Windows system, you must first download an executable package from the official Python website. Once the package is downloaded, you can install the software by double-clicking on it. For Python code development to work on some Windows systems, you may need to change the environment variables in the Control panel.

Once everything is set up as needed, open a command prompt window to see if the Python interpreter is correctly installed.

Command Prompt Code:

```
>> Python —version
```

If the command tells you what version of Python is installed, then Python is set up correctly on your system. If not, you might have to copy and paste the error into Google or use Python forums to figure out what's wrong.

Chapter 2: PyCharm and IDLE

Once you've installed Python, you'll need a development environment on your system to write programs. Even though you can work with the basic IDLE that comes with a basic Python installation, developers are encouraged to use IDEs like PyCharm for better software development workflow. IDEs make developers more productive and make it easier for them to find bugs in code that has already been turned into software.

Why Is Python Interpreter Good?

The Python interpreter is great because it is flexible and has more features than traditional compilers. For example, compared to compilers, a Python interpreter makes you wait less. Compilers run the code after it has been written and checked for mistakes. The interpreter, on the other hand, checks the code as it is being written and lets the programmer know if there is a problem before the code is run. Real-time error reporting is a good way for beginners to learn how to code while they are doing it.

When you install Python on your computer, it also installs IDLE, which stands for "Integrated development and learning environment." To start IDLE, you can type "Python" into your favorite terminal interface. The REPL mechanism is used by IDLE to show output on the computer screen. REPL is a basic method that Python interpreters use to check the lines that have been written and parse them so that they can be shown on the screen. This is done based on the input and output that is given.

Python IDLE can be a great tool for people who are just starting to learn how to code. Even though most enterprise software development is done on integrated development environments (IDEs) like PyCharm, learning some basic commands for Python IDLE can help you understand how Python interpretation works.

How to Use the Python IDLE Shell?

Once Python is installed, open a terminal or command prompt and type the following command to start the IDLE.

Command:

```
$ python
```

As shown below, when you press Enter or Return, a new shell will open.

```
>>>
```

You can test how Python IDLE works on your system by using some of the basic math or Print commands.

Program Code:

```
>>> print ("This is a sample to check that the IDLE works")
```

Output:

```
This is a sample to check that the IDLE works
```

When the Enter button is pressed, the program goes into REPL mode, and the text between the double quotes is shown on the computer screen. This is because IDLE knew that the shell window used the print() method to show strings.

You can also use math operations to test the IDLE workflow.

Program Code:

```
>>> 8 + 3
```

Output:

```
11
```

Exercise:

Use the IDLE window to check the results of other math operations, like multiplication and division.

Note:

It's important to remember that as soon as you close the terminal window, all of your code will be lost. So, even if we use an IDLE, we need to make sure that all of our code is put into a Python file.

How to Use IDLE to Open Python Files?

IDLE makes it simple to open and read Python files with a.py extension on the terminal. Keep in mind that this command will only function if you are in the same directory as the Python file.

Program Code:

```
$ python mysample.py
```

The prior command will open the previously written code for the programmers to read.

- IDLE can automatically highlight unique syntax components.
- IDLE assists developers in completing code by providing hints.
- IDLE has the ability to easily indent code.

To use any Python files on your IDLE shell, use the GUI file option and click the 'Open' button. However, advanced programmers advise using the path to open Python files if you are not in the same directory.

How to Change These Files?

Once the files are open in IDLE, you can begin editing the code in the file with your keyboard. Because IDLE provides line numbers, developers can easily manipulate any non-indented code. Once the file has been edited, press the F5 key to run it on your terminal code.

If there are no errors, the output will be displayed; otherwise, the traceback errors will be displayed.

While not as efficient as other advanced IDEs on the market, Python IDLE serves as an excellent debugging tool. It has several debugging features, including the ability to place endpoints, catch exceptions, and parse code to quickly debug the code. However, it is not ideal and may cause issues if your Project library grows.

Regardless of how little it offers, IDLE is possibly the best developer tool for complete beginners.

Exercise:

Develop a new program in Python IDLE to add two numbers and debug it with breakpoints. If you are unfamiliar with any programming components, you are free to use any Internet resources to solve this simple problem.

IDE (Integrated Development Environment)

Python IDLE is frequently not recommended for real-world application development due to its inability to handle highly demanding projects. Developers are instead asked to manage and develop their code in specialized development environments known as IDEs. Furthermore, IDEs provide programmers with tight integration capabilities with various libraries.

IDE characteristics

1. **Simple Integration into Libraries & Frameworks**

One of the important features of IDEs is that they make it simple to integrate libraries and frameworks into software applications. IDLE requires you to assign them individually each time you use them, whereas IDEs do the hard work for you by autocompleting various import statements. Many IDEs also support direct git repository integration.

2. Integration of Object-Oriented Design

Many Python programmers who create applications employ an object-oriented paradigm. Unfortunately, Python IDLE does not include any tools to help developers create applications while adhering to object-oriented principles. All modern IDEs include components such as class hierarchy diagrams to help developers get their projects started with better programming logic.

3. Syntax Highlighting

Syntax highlighting assists programmers in increasing productivity and avoiding simple, obvious errors. For example, you cannot use reserved keywords like 'if' to name variables. The IDE automatically detects this error and assists developers in understanding it through syntax highlighting.

4. Code Completion

All modern IDEs use advanced artificial intelligence and machine learning techniques to complete code for developers automatically. The IDEs gather a lot of information from the packages you use, so they can suggest different variables or methods based on your input and the logic you're writing. Even though auto-completion is a useful feature, you should never rely entirely on it because it can occasionally disrupt program execution and cause errors.

5. Version Control

Version control is a major source of frustration for developers. For example, if you use private libraries and frameworks in your application, they may occasionally be updated, causing your application to fail. As a developer, you must be aware of these changes and implement new code execution for all applications to function properly. The version control mechanism enables developers to easily update their core application without causing any disruptions to previously written code. IDEs support direct version control with websites like GitHub.

IDEs can also provide advanced debugging features for developers in addition to these features. For example, the most popular Python IDEs for independent developers and organizations are PyCharm and Eclipse. We will use PyCharm as our default IDE in this book because it is much more efficient than Eclipse and much easier to set up.

PyCharm

PyCharm is a Python-only IDE produced by JetBrains, a pioneer in software tool development. Initially, the JetBrains team created PyCharm to manage their IDEs for other programming languages. However, due to its portability, the JetBrains team later released it as a standalone product for users worldwide. PyCharm is available for all major operating systems and comes in two flavors: community and professional.

1. The community version is open-source, free software that anyone can use to write Python code. It does, however, have some limitations, particularly in terms of version control and third-party library integration.

2. The professional version is a paid IDE that offers advanced functionality and numerous integration options to developers. For example, using the professional version of PyCharm IDE, developers can easily create web or data science applications.

What Features Does PyCharm Provide?

PyCharm is well-known for its unique features for enthusiastic Python developers, as well as its high-quality integration capabilities.

1. Code Editor

PyCharm's code editor is among the best in the industry. When working with new projects in this editor, you will be astounded by the code completion abilities. Furthermore, JetBrains has used several advanced machine learning models to make the IDE intelligent enough to understand even the most complex programming blocks and provide user suggestions.

While working as a developer, the PyCharm editor can also be customized for a better viewing experience. Light and dark themes are available to users, allowing you to change the theme based on your mood.

2. Code Navigation

PyCharm's complex and comprehensive file organization system makes it simple for programmers to manage files. Bookmarks and lens mode, for example, can assist Python programmers in effectively managing their essential programming blocks and code logic.

3. Refactoring

PyCharm includes advanced refactoring features that allow developers to easily change the names of files, classes, and methods without breaking the program. When you use IDLE to refactor your code, it immediately breaks the code because the default Python IDLE is not intelligent enough to distinguish between new and old names.

When it comes to updating their code or migrating to a much better third-party library for one of their software components, most Python developers use Advanced refactoring capabilities.

4. Web Technology Integration

The majority of Python developers work in the web domain, which accounts for a sizable portion of the software industry. PyCharm simplifies the integration of developers' software with Python web frameworks such as Django. PyCharm is also intelligent enough to understand HTML, CSS, and JavaScript code, which are commonly used by web developers to create web services.

All of these features make it simple for Python web developers to integrate existing web code into a Python framework.

5. Integration With Scientific Libraries

PyCharm is also well-known for its strong support for scientific and advanced mathematical libraries like SciPy and NumPy. While it will never completely replace your data integration and cleaning setup, it will assist you in developing a basic pseudo logic for all of your data science projects.

6. Software Testing

PyCharm can execute high-level unit testing strategies for even the most complex and large projects with numerous members. It also includes advanced debugging tools and remote configuration capabilities for using the Alpha and beta testing workflows.

How to Use PyCharm?

With enough information about PyCharm, you should be convinced that it is a necessary development tool for your local system. This section contains the information you need to install PyCharm and understand how to use it to better manage your Python projects.

Step—1: Install PyCharm

PyCharm can be installed on almost any operating system. To begin, obtain the installation package from the official website or one of the numerous package managers.

Navigate to the JetBrains official website and click the downloads tab in the upper right corner. Now, depending on your operating system, download the executable or dmg file and double-click it to follow the instructions on the screen.

To download a professional version of the software, you must first provide payment information in order to download a trial version. When the trial period expires, you will be charged and will be able to use the professional version without issue.

Note:

In order for the PyCharm IDE to install successfully on your system, Python must be installed. This is because it detects the Python path and installs the software's core libraries automatically.

Step—2: Create New Projects

After installing the software, launch the PyCharm IDE from your applications or from the Desktop icon. When you open PyCharm, a new popup will appear, allowing you to start a new project from scratch. You can open a new project using the button in the upper left corner of the software interface ""File" is an option. Other options include importing and exporting existing projects or quickly saving current working projects..

When you first open a Python project, you will be prompted to choose which Python interpreter you want to use for all programming procedures. If you don't know where to look for the Python interpreter, choose 'virtualenv,' which will automatically search the system and find one for you.

Step—3: Using PyCharm to Organize

Creating new folders and resources for your Program files is essential once you begin creating projects with PyCharm.

To create a new folder on your project interface, simply select the new --> folder option. You can include any Python scripts or assets used in your software in this section.

When you create a new file in a separate folder, a file with the.py extension is created. As a result, if you want to create different class files or templates, you must do so explicitly while creating a file in your folder.

Step—4: Advanced Features in PyCharm

Once the code is written and integrated, you can use the built-in IDLE interface or the PyCharm unique output interface to run it quickly.

All code you write will be automatically saved in real-time, so you won't have to worry about losing any critical project data due to a bad network connection or power outage. To save a copy of a project on your local system, simply press Ctrl S or Cmd S.

When the program is finished, press Shift + F10 to run and compile the code with the help of an interpreter.

Using the Ctrl F or Cmd F commands, you can search for any method, variable, or snippet in your project. Simply use this shortcut and enter the information you're looking for.

Once the Python code has been imported and deployed to the required operating systems, you must begin setting up a debugging project environment in order to constantly clear bugs on your system. To place breakpoints and solve logical problems without messing up the entire code logic or breaking the core program, press Shift + F9.

Python Style Guide

Python programming grew in popularity among programmers due to the programming philosophy it supported and continues to support. Python aimed to be simple, whereas other high-level programming languages aimed to be more complex. Pearl is a great example of how this philosophy was applied and how it complicated many things for an average programmer.

Python core developers encouraged early Python adopters to adhere to a simple set of well-known principles known as '"The Zen of Python" to write code that both works and looks good. Even after twenty years, these principles are still relevant for Python programmers, and every Python programmer should be aware of them.

Enter the Python code below on the terminal to read all of these principles.

Terminal Code:

```
$ import this
```

We will go over some fundamental principles in order to better understand the philosophy that Python promotes to developers.

- Beautiful Is Better Than Ugly.

All Python programmers are encouraged to write semantically symmetrical code that is also visually appealing. Beautiful code must be well-structured; thus, programmers must write conditionals without complicating the code. Many lines of code can be made more visually appealing by employing indentation techniques. Beautifying code improves readability and can help to reduce runtime.

- Explicit Is Better Than Implicit.

For whatever reason, many developers try to conceal their programming logic, making it difficult for other programmers to understand. Python opposes this routine and encourages developers to write explicit code logic that is understandable by all. This is also one of the reasons why open-source Python frameworks and libraries are more popular.

- Simple Is Better Than Complex.

Your primary goal as a Python programmer should be to write simple code. Simplifying your code logic can help you improve your programming language skills. Your ability to write less complex code improves as you gain experience.

- Complex Is Better Than Complicated.

As with any software, there are times when you need to write complex code that solves multiple problems at once. When working on complex code, avoid making it too complicated. Using exceptions and files effectively can assist you in quickly reducing complicated code that may later turn into annoying bugs.

- There Should Be Only One Approach.

Unlike its predecessor languages, C and C++, Python advocates for consistency. As a Python programmer, you only need to use one logic for all of the instances in your program. Uniformity provides flexibility and makes it easier to maintain the code.

Chapter 3: Python Foundations

Python programmers must ensure that input is provided directly from the user and output is provided based on the inputs in order to have dynamic applications. The Python interpreter and all functions in your program can access the user's input values.

We will provide a few example programs in this chapter to help you understand how to improve the user experience of the software you have created based on input and output operations.

Why Are Input Values Required?

Application survival is dependent on input values. Everything runs on the user's input values, from web applications to the most recent metaverse applications. When you log in to Facebook, for example, you must enter your email address and password. These are inputs, and your account will be authenticated only if the information provided is correct.

Face data points are used as input in advanced applications such as facial recognition technology. Nowadays, every real-world application requests and collects user input data in order to provide a better user experience.

Use Cases:

Assume you created a Python application for a mature audience that cannot be used by anyone under the age of 18.

For the above scenario, we can use conditional input verification by asking the user to enter their age. If the user is over the age of 18, the application will become available to him or her. However, if the user is under the age of 18, the application will be inaccessible. Python evaluates whether or not someone can access your software based on inputs from all supported data types. This is just one example from the real world. There are numerous applications that can be performed by utilizing input from your end users.

Understanding the input() Function

When you call the input() function in the middle of a Python program, the interpreter will pause and wait for the user to enter the values using one of their input devices, such as a keyboard, mouse, or mobile touchscreen.

Typically, the user will provide input in response to the prompt. To create real-world applications, you must first create a good prompt GUI. This chapter will look at the text command prompts available to developers.

After entering the values, the user must press the "Enter" button on their system in order for the interpreter to resume and parse the logical programming statements used.

Example:

```
sample = input ("Which country are you from? ")
print (sample + " is a beautiful country!")
```

When the above program is run and executed, the user will first see an output prompt, as shown below.

Output:

```
Which country are you from? United States of America
United States of America is a beautiful country!
```

You can experiment by changing the input above to another country to see what happens.

Output:

```
Which country are you from? France
France is a beautiful country!
```

How To Write User Prompts?

It is recommended to use better prompts to get the user's attention when using the input() function and attempting to receive inputs from the user.

Remember not to include any extraneous information in the text. Make the prompt as straightforward as possible.

Prompt Code:

```
example = input("Which is your favorite hockey team? ")
print ("So you are a " + example + " fan. Hurray!")
```

Output:

```
Which is your favorite football team? Boston Bruins
So you are a Boston Bruins fan. Hurray!
```

You can also use the input() function to prompt the user by displaying multiple lines of strings.

Program Code:

```
prompt = "This is a simple question to find out what you like."
prompt += "\n So, please say your favorite food: "
example = input(prompt)
print (example + " is delicious")
```

Output:
```
This is a simple question to find out what you like.
So, please say your favorite food: Pasta
Pasta is delicious
```

We use the print() function to display text on the screen from the beginning of the book. The only recommended method for printing to a computer screen is print().

Any input you pass to the print() function will be converted to a string literal and displayed on the screen. While you are not required to be aware of the print() function's arguments, learning some parameters that can help you format your code is recommended.

What are String Literals?

String literals are advanced characters that can assist you in quickly formatting your data. For example, \n is a common string literal that can assist you in entering data from a new line.

Other popular string literals that can help you output data with a new tab or without whitespaces and separators are \t, \b, and \d.

What is an End Statement?

The print() function also accepts an end argument, which can be used to append any string data to the end of your string literals, as shown below.

Program Code:
```
print("Italy is a beautiful country. ", end = "Do you agree? ")
print("Yes, I do!")
```

Output:
```
Italy is a beautiful country. Do you agree? Yes, I do!
```

In the above example, "Do you agree?" is the appended text

Comments in Python

When programming teams work on complex and time-consuming projects, a lot of information must be exchanged between team members in order for the project's essence to be understood. Comments allow programmers to pass information without disrupting the program's flow.

When a programmer uses comments, the Python interpreter ignores the comments and moves on to the next line. However, because Python has a large number of open-source projects, comments assist developers in understanding how to integrate third-party libraries and frameworks into their code.

Comments make the code more readable and easier to understand. While it may appear that some programmers do not need to remember the code logic they have written, you would be surprised at how often programmers forget the code logic they have written. Having specific insights into how you wrote the code logic will be particularly useful for future reference.

Python allows programmers to use two types of comments in their code.

1. Comments on a Single Line

Single-line comments are the most commonly used type of comment by Python programmers because they can be easily written between lines of code. To use single-line comments, use the '#' symbol. Anything that comes after this symbol will be ignored by the interpreter.

Program Code:

```
# This is an example of a single-line comment followed by a print of a
        hash symbol
print ("This is an example.")
```

Output:

```
This is an example.
```

Because a single-line comment was used, the interpreter ignored it and only executed the print statement.

Why Are Single-Line Comments Important?
Single-line comments are commonly used in the middle of code to assist other programmers in understanding how the program logic works and to detail the functions of the implemented variables.

2. Comments in Multiple Lines

While it is possible to write three or four lines of continuous comments using single-line comments, it is not recommended because Python provides a better way to annotate multi-line comments. Python programmers can use string literals to create multi-line comments, as shown below.

Program Code:

```
'''

 This is a comment
 In Python
 with 4 lines
 Author: Python Best '''
print ("This is an example.")
```

Output:

```
This is an example.
```

When you run the above program, only the print statement is executed, just like single-line comments.

Why Are Multiline Comments Important?

Multiline comments are frequently used by programmers to define license details or to explain comprehensive information about various packages and methods with various implementation examples. The code can be effectively understood by the programmers who are reading it.

Reserved Keywords

Reserved keywords are programming language default keywords that programmers cannot use as identifiers while writing code. Identifiers are commonly used to name variables, classes, and functions.

The interpreter will throw an error if you use a reserved keyword in your program. For example, using 'for' for one of your variables will not work because 'for' is typically used in Python programming to define a specific type of loop structure.

There are 33 reserved keywords that you are not permitted to use in your programs. As a Python programmer, it is critical to avoid making unnecessary mistakes when working on complex projects.

Exercise:

Using the Python terminal, try to find the reserved keywords in Python to become familiar with the Python commands we discussed previously.

Operators are commonly used by computer programmers to combine literal and form statements or expressions.

Example:

$$2x + 3z = 34$$

Here, 2x, 3z, and 34 are literals, and + and = are operators that are applied to these literals to form an expression.

Operators in Python

In mathematics, operators are first used to form mathematical expressions. The first programmers used these operators and the basic programming components to easily assign and manipulate values. Operators can be combined with any number of literal values to form complex expressions that can aid programmers in the implementation of difficult algorithms.

Example:

```
a = 18
b = 20
print(a + b)
```

Output:

38

a and b are the operands, whereas = and + are operators that are used.

Different Types of Operators

Programmers can use different types of operators to implement various types of programming logic. The most commonly used operators are arithmetic operators, which assist programmers in applying mathematical logic to various literals, such as variables, in their code.

The arithmetic operators that a Python programmer needs to know to write better programming structures are addition, subtraction, multiplication, and division.

1. Addition

To add two literals to a program, use the addition operator. These literals can be variables or lists, and they can sometimes be data of two different data types. The Python interpreter is smart enough to recognize two different data types and return a result to the programmer. The addition operation is represented by the symbol '+'.

Program Code:

```
x = 26
y = 15
z = x + y
# + is the addition operator
print(z)
```

When the program runs using an IDE or IDLE, the interpreter will add the two variable values and assign them into the variable z, as specified by the developer.

Output:

41

2. Subtraction Operator

The subtraction operator is used to subtract two literals. These literals can be variables or lists, and they can sometimes be data of two different data types. - is the symbol for the subtraction operation.

Program Code:

```
x = 26
y = 15
z = x - y
# - is the subtraction operator
print(z)
```

When the program is executed using an IDE or IDLE, the interpreter will find the difference between the two variable values and input it into z as specified by the developer.

Output:

```
11
```

3. Multiplication Operator

The multiplication operator computes the product of two literals. These literals can be variables or lists, and they can sometimes be data of two different data types. The symbol * represents a multiplication operation.

Program Code:

```
x = 6
y = 4
z = x * y
# * is the multiplication operator
print(z)
```

When the program runs in an IDE or IDLE, the interpreter will find the product of the two variable values and enter it into the z variable as specified by the developer.

Output:

```
24
```

4. Division Operator

In a program, the division operator is used to find the division quotient of two literals. The quotient can also be calculated using floating-point numbers, and the division symbol "/" is used.

Program Code:

```
x = 8
y = 4
z = x / y
# / is the division operator
print(z)
```

When the program runs in an IDE or IDLE, the interpreter will find the quotient of the two variable values and enter it into the z variable as specified by the developer.

Output:

```
2.0
```

5. Modulus

Modulus is typically used to calculate the remainder of a division operation. The modulus operator can be used to implement a wide range of programming logic, and% is the modulus operation symbol.

Program Code:

```
x = 9
y = 4
z = x % y
# % is the modulus operator
print(z)
```

When the program is executed using an IDE or IDLE, the interpreter will find the remainder of the two variable values and input them into z as specified by the developer.

Output:

```
1
```

The quotient in this case is 2.25, but the remainder is 1, as shown in the program output. You can use floor division operations instead of displaying floating-point numbers as a quotient for division operations.

6. Floor Division

Floor division is an alternative arithmetic operator that developers frequently use when they are not concerned with the precision of the result. The nearest integer for the quotient obtained after a division operation is usually displayed by this operator.

"//" is the symbol for a floor division operator.

Program Code:

```
x = 9
y = 4
z = x // y
# This is the floor division operator
print (z)
```

Output:

```
2
```

The above program has a Quotient of 2.25. However, because we are using the floor division operator, the program has returned the nearest integer.

7. Bitwise Operators

Bitwise operators are advanced operators that developers frequently use to perform special features such as compression, encryption, and error detection.

Bitwise operators of various types are used in all high-level programming languages.

1. AND (&)

2. OR (|)

3. XOR (^)

4. NOT (~)

All these bitwise operators follow the same principles as logical operators in mathematics.

Operator Precedence

Because there are different operators and mathematical expressions are formed by combining them, dealing with advanced mathematical expressions to create real-world applications can quickly become complex. Operator precedence provides programmers with clear objectives for prioritizing which operators perform a mathematical operation.

If a developer fails to follow operator precedence rules, the values may change completely, resulting in application crashes.

Operator Precedence Rules in Python:

- In any mathematical expression you deal with in Python, precedence takes precedence. As a result, if operators are enclosed by parenthesis, the interpreter will address them first and then move on to the others.

- Bitwise operators are usually given second precedence.

- The mathematical operators used for multiplication and division are given the highest priority. The operators that must be preferred in the same order are *, /, %, and //.

- The remaining arithmetic operations, such as addition and subtraction, take precedence. These operators are represented by the symbols + and -.

- Comparison and logical operators have final operator precedence.

Exercises

1. Create a program that asks the user for two numbers and performs addition, subtraction, multiplication, and division operations using these numbers. Print the results of each operation.

2. Create a program that asks the user for two numbers and checks if the first number is equal to, greater than, or less than the second number. Print the results of each comparison.

3. Create a program that asks the user for three numbers and checks if all of them are positive, or at least one of them is negative. Print the result of the logical operation.

4. Create a program that asks the user fort three numbers and check for each number if it divisible by 3, 4, or 7. Print the result each time.

5. Write a program that asks the user to input two numbers and then performs both a modulus and floor division operation on those numbers. Print the results of both operations to the screen.

Chapter 4: **Python Variables**

To function properly, Python programs require basic components like variables and operators. These elements, including variables and operators, are simple for novice programmers to comprehend and apply, allowing them to develop algorithms necessary for creating sophisticated software.

What are Variables in Python?

Variables are a way to store and handle data in a Python program. They allow both users and the software to interact with the data. Without data, software applications are useless and serve no purpose for end-users.

Variables are used in Python to store data in a specific computer memory location, allowing the software to upload or download data. The concept of variables was first used in Algebra and have been a fundamental part of high-level programming languages since their inception.

For example, in the mathematical equation $2x + 3y$, the variables x and y can be assigned values, which can then be used to change the output of the equation. In programming, variables with unchanging values are referred to as constants. To understand how variables work in Python, it's important to understand the execution of Python programs, which can be demonstrated through a print statement.

In the same way, by using variables, you can modify the output of a program by supplying literal values. Variables are replaceable, while values that shouldn't be replaced are often referred to as constants in programming.

To grasp how variables function, one needs to comprehend the execution process of Python programs. A print statement will help illustrate this.

Example:

Program Code:

```
print("This is a sentence.")
```

Output:

```
This is a sentence.
```

The code instantly displays the output once the print statement is executed. But there is much more happening behind the scenes.

What happens?

- The program reads each line and matches with libraries it has access to.
- An interpreter performs this matching process, using high parsing abilities to identify each character in the program, match variable details, and retrieve information from memory locations to validate the program's logic.
- Despite complex parsing, the program will raise errors if the interpreter cannot find defined methods or variables.
- In the above example, the interpreter recognizes the print statement as a core library method in Python and outputs any string literals in parenthesis.

If you understand the explanation, it is now time to learn about variables in Python.

Program Code:

```
program = " This is a sentence."
print (program)
```

Output:

```
This is a sentence.
```

What Happened?

- At the onset of the program execution, the interpreter will typically parse every line of code given by the programmer.
- Instead of just encountering a print statement followed by text, the interpreter now sees a special identifier referred to as a variable named 'program.' The interpreter checks prior code and discovers that the variable is defined with text and saved at a specific memory location.
- Subsequently, the interpreter will display the variable on the screen as directed by the programmer by retrieving the information defined within the variable.
- This is the fundamental process by which variables work, even in complicated code logic.

Variables can change instantly when they are substituted. It is important for a Python programmer to be aware of this because dynamic programs frequently alter variables according to user inputs and replace them even as the program operates in real-time.

Program Code:

```
sample = "My first example"
print(sample)
sample = "My second example"
print(sample)
```

Output:

```
My first example
```

```
My second example
```

Since we know that the Python interpreter parses the code line by line sequentially, the first statement in the previous example is printed with the first variable value provided, and the second print statement is printed with the second variable value provided.

How to Name Variables

When creating variables, all Python programmers must follow the Python community's default guidelines. Failure to follow these conditions will result in difficult-to-ignore errors or, in rare cases, application crash. Using a specific guideline when developing programs can also help to improve readability.

Rules for keep in mind:

- Python guidelines specify that variable names can only contain numbers, alphabetical characters, and an underscore. So, for example, 'sample1' can be used as a variable name, whereas '$sample1' cannot because it begins with the unsupported symbol $.

- Python programmers can't begin a variable name with a number. For example, 'sample1' is a valid variable naming format, whereas '1sample' is not.

- Python programmers can't use reserved words assigned to various Python programming routines. Currently, developers cannot use 33 reserved keywords as identifiers when developing real-world Python applications. For example, the keyword 'for' is reserved.

- While this is not a hard and fast rule, it is always preferable to use a simple variable naming method for improved readability. Using complex or confusing variable names can make your code appear sloppy. While this is a good practice for other high-level languages such as C, C++, and Pearl, Python does not support it.

How to Define Variables

All variables defined in the Python programming language begin with the assignment operator (=) to assign a value to the variable.

Syntax Format:

Name_of_the_variable = Value_of_the_variable

Example:

```
example = 123
# This is a variable with an integer data type
example1 = "USA"
```

```
# This is a variable with a string data type
```

In this case, "example" is the name of the variable we created, and 343 is the variable value we assigned to it when it was created.

Consider the variable-defining method above, where we did not explicitly mention any variable data type because Python is intelligent enough to understand variable data types on its own.

How to Determine the Memory Address of a Variable

All variables are kept in a separate memory location. The Python interpreter will pull the information from this memory location whenever you call the variable name. When you ask the Python interpreter to replace a variable, it will simply take the previously placed variable value and replace it with the new variable value. The old variable value will be deleted or saved for future use cases using a garbage mechanism.

Pointers are commonly used in programming languages such as C to quickly determine and pull information about a variable's memory location. Python, on the other hand, does not support pointers because it is often difficult to implement and requires many compilation skills that the interpreter is usually unaware of. Instead, Python developers can use the built-in id() function to quickly obtain the variable's memory address.

Program Code:

```
# First, let's create a variable with an integer data type
sample = 32
# Now let's call its memory address using the built-in function id()
address = id(sample)
print(address)
```

Output:

```
1x10744488x
```

In this case, 1x10744488x is the variable's hexadecimal memory location.

Using the method below, you can now replace the variable and see if the id() has changed.

Program Code:

```
# Let's assign a value to the variable 'sample' and print its address
sample = 64
print(id(sample))
# Now we replace the variable value with a new one
sample = 78
```

```
# This will again print the output of the memory location address
print(id(sample))
```

Output:

```
1x10744488x
1x10744488x
```

Although the memory location did not change, a small print verification (print(sample)) is sufficient to see that the variable value has changed.

Local and Global Variables

Variables can be both local and global, depending on your programming logic. Local variables, in theory, can only be used in the methods or classes that you specify. Global variables, on the other hand, can be used in any part of the program without issue. When you call a local variable outside of a function, the Python interpreter will usually throw an error.

Program Code:

```
# This is an example of a local variable within a function
def mysample():
    x = "This is a sentence"
    print(x)
mysample()
```

Output:

```
This is a sentence
```

In this example, the variable is defined as a local variable within a function. As a result, whenever you call it from within a function, it will throw a traceback error, as shown below.

Program Code:

```
# This is an example of function with a local variable
def sample():
    x = "This is a sentence"
    print(x)
# This is another function
def secondsample():
    print(example)

sample()
secondsample()
```

Output:

```
This is a sentence
NameError: name 'x' is not defined
```

Global variables, on the other hand, can be used to initiate variables for the entire program.

Program Code:

```python
# Let's create a global variable
x = "This is a sentence"

# Let's initialize two methods
def method1():
    print(x)

def method2():
    print(x)

# Let's call them
method1()
method2()
```

Output:

```
This is a sentence
This is a sentence
```

Since both functions can access global variables, two print statements are displayed on the computer screen.

It is entirely up to you to decide which type of variables to use. Many programmers rely heavily on local variables to make their applications run faster. Global variables, on the other hand, can be used if you don't want to be overwhelmed with memory management.

Chapter 5: Data Types in Python

Python programmers use a wide range of data types to build cross-platform applications. As a result, a Python programmer must understand the significance of data types in software development.

What exactly are Data Types?

To be more specific, data types are a set of predefined values that programmers use when creating variables. It is also important to remember that because Python is not a statically typed language, it is not necessary to explicitly define variable data types. All statically typed languages, such as C and C++, typically require programmers to define variable data types.

While Python programmers are not required to define them in order to create programs, understanding the various available data types is still necessary for developing complex programs that can interact with users efficiently.

Here's an example of a statically typed language and how variables are defined.

Program Code:

```
int years = 12;
```

In this case, int is the defined data type, years is the variable's name, and 12 is the value supplied to be stored in the age variable.

Python, on the other hand, defines a variable without explicitly defining the variable type, as illustrated below.

Program Code:

```
years = 12
```

years and value are provided here. However, the data type is not defined because the Python interpreter understands that the value provided is an integer.

Different Data Types

Before we get into the various data types that Python supports, let's talk about the basic programming fragments that developers use to create logical statements while programming.

Let's see a simple expression and statement. To make logical statements in a programming language, three main components are used.

1. Data identifiers

To store data, programming components such as variables, lists, and tuples are created.

For example:

```
a = 24
```

x is a variable in this programming fragment that was created to store sequential data.

2. Literals

These are the values assigned to any data fragments created by a program.

For Example:

```
a = 24
```

In this programming fragment, **24** is the literal assigned to the newly created data fragment.

3. Operators

Operators implement mathematical operations while developing code for real-world applications.

For Example:

```
a = 24
```

The assignment operator = is used in the preceding code. Other arithmetic operators, such as +, -, *, and /, are well-known for producing logical Python code.

We'll go over some of the most common data types used by Python programmers in their applications.

Strings

Strings are data types that are commonly used to represent a large amount of text. String data types, for example, can be used to represent text in a program by linking them with single quotes. When a string data type is created, an 'str' object with a sequence of characters is created.

Text messages are the most common way for humans to communicate with one another. As a result, strings are the most important data types for developers to understand in order to create meaningful software. It is also critical to represent data in strings because computers only understand binary data. As a result, using ASCII and Unicode encoding mechanisms is critical.

Python 3 introduced an advanced encoding mechanism for understanding foreign languages such as Chinese, Japanese, and Korean, making Strings indispensable for software development.

In what way are strings represented?

```
z = 'This is my sentence'
print (z)
```

Output:

```
This is my sentence
```

Everything between the single quotation marks is a string data type. The variable 'x' is used to define this string data. The number of bits a variable occupies usually determines its memory location and size when it has a string data type. A string data type's number of characters is directly proportional to its bit count.

In the preceding example, 'This is an example' has 18 characters, including whitespaces.

As a Python programmer, you have several other options for defining strings. When working on real-world projects, use a single type whenever possible for consistency.

Program Code:

```
# Double quotes to define strings
a = "This is my sentence"
print(a)

# Three single quotes to define strings
b = '''This is my sentence'''
print(b)

# Three double quotes to define strings
c = """This is my sentence
 but with more than one line """
print(c)
```

Output:

```
This is my sentence
This is my sentence
This is my sentence
 but with more than one line
```

In the previous example, we defined three methods for defining strings. Special characters, symbols, and new tab lines can also be used between quotes. Python also supports escape sequences, which are used by all programming languages. For example, n is a popular escape sequence used by programmers to create new lines.

How Do I Access Characters in Strings?

Because strings are the most commonly used data types in Python, the core library includes several built-in functions for interacting with string data. To access characters in a string, you must first know the index numbers. Index numbers typically begin with 0 rather than 1. Negative indexing and slicing operations can also be used to access a portion of a string.

Example:

```
# We first create a string to access its characters
s = 'PYTHON'

# We print the whole string
print ('Whole string =', s)

# We print the first character
print ('1st character =', s[0])

# We print the last character using negative indexing
print ('Last character =', s[-1])

# We print the last character using positive indexing
print ('Again, Last character =', s[5])

# We print the first 2 characters (index 0 to 1)
print ('Sliced character =', s[0:2])
```

Output:

```
Whole string = PYTHON
1st character = P
Last character = N
Again, Last character = N
Sliced character = PY
```

Because all string data types are immutable, it is impossible to replace characters in a literal string. As a result, attempting to replace string characters will result in a Type error.

Program Code:

```
s = 'PYTHON'
s[1] = 'c'
print(s)
```

Output:

```
TypeError: 'str' object does not support item assignment
```

String Formatting

With the modulus (%) operator, Python makes it simple to format your string. It is known as *string formatting operator*.

Program Code:

```
print ("Today I have eaten %d apples" %3)
```

Output:

```
Today I have eaten 4 apples
```

You can use %d to format integers. You can also use %s to format your text.

String Manipulation Techniques

Because strings are the most commonly used data type, the Python core library provides several manipulation techniques for programmers to use. Understanding string manipulation techniques will help you in quickly extracting data from a large pool of data. These techniques are more widely known among data scientists.

1. Concatenate

Concatenation is the joining of two distinct entities. Using the arithmetic operator '+,' two strings can be joined together using this procedure. If you want to improve string readability, simply use whitespaces between the two strings.

Program Code:

```
example = 'Today is' + 'a wonderful day'
print (example)
```

Output:

```
Today isa wonderful day
```

Remember that whitespaces are not allowed when concatenating. While concatenating, you must add whitespaces on your own, as shown below.

Program Code:

```
example = 'Today is' + ' ' + 'a wonderful day'
print (example)
```

Output:

```
Today is a wonderful day
```

2. Multiply

When you use the String multiply technique, your string value is continuously repeated. The * operator can be used to multiply string content.

Program Code:

```
example = 'Yes '* 4
print(example)
```

Output:

```
Yes Yes Yes Yes
```

3. Appending

You can use this operation to add any string to the end of another string by using the arithmetic operator +=. Keep in mind that the appended string will only be added at the end of the string, not in the middle.

Program Code:

```
example = "Today is a beautiful day "
example += "to start learning Python!"
print (example)
```

Output:

```
Today is a beautiful day to start learning Python!
```

4. Length

In addition to string operations, you can use prebuilt functions in the core library to perform additional tasks in your code. The 'length()' function, for example, returns the number of characters in a string.

Blank Space will be added as a character in the string as well.

Program Code:

```
x = 'Tomorrow it will be sunny'
print(len(x))
```

Output:

```
25
```

5. Find

When you use strings as your primary data type, there will be times when you need to find a specific part of the string. To solve this problem, you can use the built-in find() function. The output will provide an index for the position the first time the input is found so you can verify.

When you use the find() function in Python, the interpreter will only return positive indexes.

Program Code:

```
x = 'Tomorrow it will be sunny'
y = x.find('it')
print(y)
```

Output:

```
9
```

If the substring is not found, the interpreter will return a value of -1.

Program Code:

```
x = 'Tomorrow it will be sunny'
y = x.find('hi')
print(y)
```

Output:

```
-1
```

6. Lower and upper case

lower() and higher() functions can be used to convert characters in a string to completely lower or upper case.

Program Code:

```
example = "Asia is the biggest continent"
sample = example.lower()
print(sample)
```

Output:

```
asia is the biggest continent
```

Program Code:

```
example = "Asia is the biggest continent"
sample = example.upper()
print(sample)
```

Output:

```
ASIA IS THE BIGGEST CONTINENT
```

7. Title

To convert string format to camel case format, use the title() function.

Program Code:

```
example = "Asia is the biggest continent"
sample = example.title()
print(sample)
```

Output:

```
Asia Is The Biggest Continent
```

Integers

In Python, integers are special data types that allow you to include integer numbers in your code. To perform arithmetic operations or to provide information about a statistical value, numerical values are required.

When a Python interpreter encounters a data value of the integer type, it creates an int object with the value provided. Because int object values are not immutable, they can be replaced whenever the developer desires.

'Int' data types are used by developers to create a variety of complex features in their software. Integers are commonly used to represent the pixel density value of an image or video file.

It is important for a developer to understand the unary operators (+,-), which can be used to represent positive and negative integers, respectively. The unary operator does not need to be specified for positive integers (+), but it must be included for negative integers.

Program Code:

```
x = 13
y = -92
print(x)
print(y)
```

Output:

```
13
-92
```

Python can handle numbers with up to ten digits. While most real-world applications do not cause bottlenecks due to larger numerical values, it's better to be sure that no huge integers are involved.

Floating—Point numbers

All numerical values are not integers. You may occasionally need to work with data with a decimal value. Python ensures that developers deal with this data using floating-point numbers. With floating-point numbers, you can work with decimal values up to ten decimal points long.

Program Code:

```
x = 3.121212
y = 58.4545
print(x)
print(y)
```

Output:

```
3.121212
58.4545
```

Floating-point numbers can also be used to represent data in hexadecimal notation.

Program Code:

```
x = float.hex(15.2698)
print(x)
```

Output:

```
0x1.e8a2339c0ebeep+3
```

Python programmers also commonly use floating-point data types to represent complex and exponential numbers.

Boolean Data Type

Booleans are special data types that are typically used to represent a True or False value when comparing two different values.

Program Code:

```
A = 21
B = 55
print (A > B)
```

Output:

```
False
```

Because the value of A is not greater than the value of B in the preceding example, the output is False. When dealing with logical operations, Boolean data types come in handy.

Chapter 6: Advanced Data Structures in Python

Python programmers frequently deal with large amounts of data, so using variables all the time is not a good idea. Data Scientists, in particular, who frequently deal with large amounts of data, may become overwhelmed by the volume of dynamic data they must deal with. As a result, when working on complex and data-intensive projects, it is critical to use the lists option provided by Python's core library. These are similar to data structures such as arrays found in core programming languages such as C and C++.

Understanding the various data structures provided by Python, as well as learning techniques to add or modify data using these data structures, is a must for any Python programmer.

Lists

Lists are Python data types that allow you to add different data types sequentially. Lists have all of the same properties as variables. They can be easily replaced, passed, or manipulated with the help of the Python core library's methods.

In Python, lists are typically represented as follows:

[22, 23, 24]

The list elements here are 22, 23, and 24. It is also important to understand that all list elements are of integer data type and are not explicitly defined because the Python interpreter can detect their data type.

In the above format, lists begin and end with a square bracket. A comma will be used to separate all of the elements in the list. It's also worth noting that if the elements in a list are of the string data type, they're usually surrounded by quotes. All of the elements in a list are also referred to as items.

Example:

[Alaska, California, Alabama]

Alaska, California, and Alabama are referred to as list elements in this context. As an example, all of the lists can be assigned to a variable. When you print the variable, the list will be printed like any other data type.

Program Code:

```
x = ['Alaska', 'California', 'Alabama']
print(x)
```

Output:

```
['Alaska', 'California', 'Alabama']
```

Empty List

If a Python list has no elements, it is referred to as an empty list. An empty list is also known as a null list. It's usually written as [].

Program Code:

```
# This is an empty list
emptylist = []
```

List Indexing

Python makes it simple to manipulate or replace the elements of a list, specifically through the use of indexes. Indexes typically begin with 0 and provide Python programmers with numerous functions, such as "slicing" and "searching," to ensure that their programs run smoothly.

Assume we have a list that we have previously used. We will print each element on the computer screen using the indexes.

Program Code:

```
myList = ['California', 'Alaska', 'Alabama']
print(myList[0])
print(myList[1])
print(myList[2])
```

Output:

```
'California'
'Alaska'
'Alabama'
```

In the previous example, when the Python interpreter detects 0 as an index, it prints the first element. As the index rises, so does the position on the list.

The items in the list can also be called as shown below, along with a string literal.

Program Code:

```
myList = ['California', 'Alaska', 'Alabama']
print(myList [1] + ' is a wonderful state')
```

Output:

```
California is a wonderful state
```

If you provide an index value that is greater than the number of list elements present, an index error will be returned.

Program Code:

```
myList = ['California', 'Alaska', 'Alabama']
print(myList [3])
```

Output:

```
IndexError: list index out of range
```

Note: It is also important to remember that the floating-point number cannot be used as an index value.

Program Code:

```
myList = ['California', 'Alaska', 'Alabama']
print(myList [2.2])
```

Output:

```
TypeError: list indices must be integers or slices, not float
```

As shown below, all lists can have other lists as elements. Child lists are all the lists contained within a list.

Program Code:

```
x = [[5,123,4],56,32,14]
print(x)
```

Output:

```
[[5, 123, 4], 56, 32, 14]
```

You can call the elements in the child list using the 'list [][]' format.

Program Code:

```
x = [[5,123,4],56,32,14]
print(x[0][1])
```

Output:

```
123
```

In the previous example, the second element of the nested list is 123, which is displayed as output. The elements of a list can also be referred to using the negative index. Typically, -1 denotes the last index, whereas -2 denotes the element preceding the last element.

Program Code:

```
myList = ['California', 'Alaska', 'Alabama']
print(myList [-1])
```

Output:

```
Alabama
```

You've already learned about how lists are represented. In the following section, we will discuss some of the functions that can be manipulated using a list data structure.

Slicing Using Lists

Slicing lists allows programmers to avoid dealing with an overwhelming number of elements contained within a list. By slicing, you can focus only on the part of a list that is relevant to your program logic.

Syntax:

Listname[start of the index : end of the index]

A colon is typically used to separate the beginning and ending indexes of the list that you want to slice.

Program Code:

```
myList = [23,34,78,94,54]
print(myList[1:3])
```

Output:

```
[34, 78]
```

You do not need to enter the list's beginning or end when slicing the list elements. If it is not entered, the interpreter will assume it is the first or last element in the list.

Program Code:

```
myList = [23,34,78,94,54]
print(myList[:3])
```

Output:

```
[23, 34, 78]
```

Because the slice value before the semicolon was not provided in the previous example, the interpreter assumed it came from the first element.

Program Code:

```
myList = [23,34,78,94,54]
print(myList[3:])
```

Output:

```
[94, 54]
```

In this example, the interpreter has assumed that the value following the semicolon represents the end of the list. If neither value is provided, the entire list is returned, as shown below.

Program Code:

```
myList = [23,34,78,94,54]
print(myList[:])
```

Output:

```
[23, 34, 78, 94, 54]
```

Get list length

To quickly determine the length of a list, use the built-in len() function.

Program Code:

```
myList = [23,34,78,94,54]
print(len(myList))
```

Output:

```
5
```

Changing Values of a List

As shown below, you can easily change the values inside a list using the assignment operator.

Program Code:

```
myList = [23,34,78,94,54]
myList [3] = 58
print(myList)
```

Output:

```
[23, 34, 78, 58, 54]
```

You can also replace a list value with an already existing list value, as shown below.

Program Code:

```
myList = [23,34,78,94,54]
myList [3] = myList[2]
print(myList)
```

Output:

```
[23, 34, 78, 78, 54]
```

Concatenating Lists

The Arithmetic operator '+' can be used to easily combine two lists.

Program Code:

```
myList = [23,34,78,94,54]
x = [1,2,3]
print(myList + x)
```

Output:

```
[23, 34, 78, 94, 54, 1, 2, 3]
```

Replication of a List

Using the '*' operator, you can quickly multiply list elements with this function.

Program Code:

```
print([1,2,3] * 4)
```

Output:

```
[1, 2, 3, 1, 2, 3, 1, 2, 3, 1, 2, 3]
```

Element Deletion

Using the 'del' statement, you can easily remove an element from a list.

Program Code:

```
myList = [12,13,14,15,16,17]
del(myList [2])
print(myList)
```

Output:

```
[12, 13, 15, 16, 17]
```

Using the operators "in" and "not in"

Using the logical operators 'in' and 'not in,' Python makes it simple to determine whether a list element is present or not in a list. As a result, this function returns either a True or False Boolean value.

Program Code:

```
colors = ['yellow', 'orange', 'blue']
x = 'orange' in colors
print(x)
```

Output:

```
True
```

index()

Using the index() list function, you can quickly determine the index position of a list element.

Program Code:

```
x = [12, 45, 78]
print(x.index(45))
```

Output:

```
1
```

If you provide a list element that does not exist within a list, you will receive a type error.

Program Code:

```
x = [12, 45, 78]
print(x.index(49))
```

Output:

```
ValueError: 49 is not in list
```

insert()

You can insert a new element to the list at any position in the list by using the insert() function.

Syntax:

insert(index position, 'item')

Program Code:

```
x = [12, 45, 78]
x.insert(2,11)
print(x)
```

Output:

```
[12, 45, 11, 78]
```

The third element is moved to the fourth position and the new element is added to the third

sort()

Python developers can easily arrange all the elements in a list using either ascending or descending order by using the sort() function.

Program Code:

```python
x = [78, 12, 45]
x.sort()
print(x)
```

Output:

```
[12, 45, 78]
```

If you use strings in the list, the list will be sorted alphabetically.

Program Code:

```python
x = ['yellow', 'blue', 'orange', 'grey']
x.sort()
print(x)
```

Output:

```
['blue', 'grey', 'orange', 'yellow']
```

Tuples

Even though lists are popular data structures that Python programmers frequently use in their applications, they have several implementation issues. Because all lists created with Python are mutual objects, they are simple to replace, delete, or manipulate.

As a software developer, you may be required to keep immutable lists that cannot be altered in any way. That's why tuples exist. Within Tuples, it is not possible to change initiated elements in any way. When you try to change the content of a tuple, you will get a "Type Error" message.

Program Code:

```python
# Let's create a tuple using Python
t = ('Cat', 'Tree', 'Apple')
print(t)
```

Output:

```
('Cat', 'Tree', 'Apple')
```

In the previous example, we simply initiated a tuple and used a print function to display it on the screen. Tuples, unlike lists, are not represented with square brackets, but rather with parenthesis to distinguish them from lists.

To understand how tuples work, try changing one of the elements in the preceding example and printing the tuple to see what happens.

Program Code:

```python
t = ('Cat', 'Tree', 'Apple')
```

```
print(t)

# Trying to replace an element in the tuple...
t[2] = 'Mango'
print(t)
```

Output:

```
('Cat', 'Tree', 'Apple')
TypeError: 'tuple' object does not support item assignment
```

In the previous example, if a tuple element is changed, the interpreter will throw an error. This demonstrates that all tuple elements are immutable and cannot be replaced, deleted, or added.

Tuples Concatenation

Tuples, like the many list operations we've seen, can be used to work on specific operations. For example, just like lists, you can use Python to add or multiply the elements in a tuple.

Program Code:

```
tuple1 = (17,18,19)
tuple2 = (16,19,28)
# Adding two tuples
print(tuple1 + tuple2)
```

Output:

```
(17, 18, 19, 16, 19, 28)
```

The Addition operator is used to concatenate two tuples in the preceding example. Similarly, you can use the multiplication operator to quickly increase the elements in your tuple. We can also nest tuples within tuples. This is commonly referred to as nesting tuples.

Program Code:

```
X = (1,2,3)
Y = ('Orange','Apple','Banana')
Z = (X,Y)
print(Z)
```

Output:

```
((1, 2, 3), ('Orange', 'Apple', 'Banana'))
```

Two tuples are nested within another tuple in the previous example.

Replication

When working with lists, you can use the * operator to repeat the values.

Program Code:

```
T = (4,5,6) * 4
print(T)
```

Output:

```
(4, 5, 6, 4, 5, 6, 4, 5, 6, 4, 5, 6)
```

As previously stated, changing the values of tuples is impossible because they are designed to be immutable. Here is what happens if we try to swap one value for another.

Program Code:

```
T = (45,78,89)
T[2] = 15
print(T)
```

Output:

```
TypeError: 'tuple' object does not support item assignment
```

Slicing With Tuples

The slicing technique, which uses indexes to extract a portion of the tuple, makes it simple to slice a portion of the tuple.

Program Code:

```
t = (24,25,26,27,28,29,30)
print(t[2:4] )
```

Output:

```
(26, 27)
```

Tuple Deletion

It is not possible to delete a specific element from a tuple, but it is possible to delete the entire tuple using the command below. This is true for any type of variable.

Program Code:

```
t = (24,25,26,27,28,29,30)
del t
print(t)
```

Output:

```
NameError: name 't' is not defined
```

Dictionaries

values as pairs rather than single values as lists and tuples do. The "key: value" pair is used by dictionaries to ensure that the data provided is more optimized and works better. Dictionaries are also represented by curly brackets, which distinguishes them from lists and tuples.

How Do I Create a Dictionary?

As previously stated, dictionaries are defined using key: value pairs separated by commas. The elements will be placed in a sequential order and must be separated.

Syntax:

Dictionary_sample = { key: value , key: value ....) }

As a developer, you can add an unlimited number of key:value pairs to a dictionary.

Example:

```
Capitals = {'France': 'Paris', 'Spain': 'Madrid', 'Italy': 'Rome'}
print(Capitals)
```

Output:

```
{'France': 'Paris', 'Spain': 'Madrid', 'Italy': 'Rome'}
```

You can also build a nested dictionary. A nested dictionary is a dictionary within a dictionary:

```
Capitals = {'France': 'Paris', 'Spain': 'Madrid', 'Italy': 'Rome',
        'Australia': {'Melbourne', 'Sydney'}}
print(Capitals)
```

Output:

```
{'France': 'Paris', 'Spain': 'Madrid', 'Italy': 'Rome', 'Australia':
        {'Sydney', 'Melbourne'}}
```

The last key: pair value in the second example has a dictionary with two key: pair values.

Exercises

1. List exercise: Create a list of 5 numbers and then print the sum and average of the numbers.

2. Create a tuple of 5 names and then print the first and last name.

3. Create a dictionary with 5 key-value pairs and then print the value of the third key.

4. Create a list with 5 fruits (e.g., apples, bananas, etc.). Ask the user to input a fruit. Check if the fruit is in the list. If the fruit is in the list, display a message saying "The fruit is in the list." If the fruit is not in the list, display a message saying "The fruit is not in the list."

5. Create a list with 3 colors. Then ask the user to give a color as input. If the color is in the list, display a message saying so. Otherwise, append the color given by the user to the end of the list and print the updated list

Chapter 7: Conditionals and Loops

Any computer program must make decisions for real-world application. A mobile application with advanced software, for example, will use your inputs to display whatever you want. While using a mobile or web application, the user makes decisions. The program must be intelligent enough to provide a relevant interface based on the user's selection. This dynamic thinking is very similar to human thinking.

When writing in Python, you must be aware of conditionals and loops to ensure that your programs mimic these conditions. These are high-level programming structures that can make your Python programs more effective.

Conditionals and loops can also help you reduce the execution time of your programs, making them run faster. A Python programmer who wants to work with well-known teams should be aware of these techniques, as they are also prerequisite requirements for more advanced topics such as Functions and Modules, which we will discuss further.

Comparison Operators

To practically understand conditionals and loops , you must be aware of the various comparison operators supported by Python as a programming language.

Comparison operators, also known as relational operators, typically compare two operands to each other and return a Boolean value, either True or False.

Note: 'True' and 'False' are special Boolean values supported by Python to assist programs in making relevant decisions. Boolean values are the basic of logic gates present within microprocessors.

1. **Less than (<) operator**

This operator determines whether the left operand value is less than the right operand value.

Program Code:

```
print(12 < 19)
```

Output:

```
True
```

Program Code:

```
print(87 < 36)
```

Output:

```
False
```

If you look at the two examples above, you'll notice that the first has a 'True' output because 12 is less than 19, while the second has a 'False' output because 87 is not less than 36.

With a less-than operator, you can apply the same principle to floating-point values.

Program Code:

```
a = 9.5 < 10.26
print(a)
```

Output:

```
True
```

To compare strings in ASCII format, you can also use the "less than" operator.

Program Code:

```
a = 'Banana' < 'banana'
print(a)
```

Output:

```
True
```

Because the ASCII value of lowercase letters is higher than that of uppercase letters, the Boolean value in the previous example is True.

Exercise:

Determine the ASCII sum for the word 'banana' mentioned above.

These relational operators can also be applied to other data structures, such as tuples. Before comparing, however, ensure that all of the values in a tuple are of the same data type.

Program Code:

```
print((15,18,98) < (25,48,18,19))
```

Output:

```
True
```

If the tuples have different data types, an error message will appear on the terminal.

Program Code:

```
print((20,30,40) < ('three',4,5))
```

Output:

```
TypeError: '<' not supported between instances of 'int' and 'str'
```

2. Greater than (>) operator

A *greater than* operator is typically used to determine whether the left operand value is greater than the right operand value.

Program Code:

```
print(32 > 56)
```

Output:

```
False
```

The Boolean value in the first example is False because the right operand value 32 is less than 56.

The same relational operator can also be used with floating-point values and other data types, such as tuples.

3. Equal (== operator)

An *equal* operator determines whether the values of the right and left operands are equal. If the operand values are the same, the Boolean value is True. Otherwise, it's False.

Program Code:

```
print(5 == 5)
```

Output:

```
True
```

Program Code:

```
print(12 == 21)
```

Output:

```
False
```

Control Flow Statements

With a solid understanding of comparison operators under your belt, you are now ready to learn about the various control statements that are required of all Python developers. Control flow statements are commonly used by programmers to write simple code for beginners.

Sequential Structure

All of your program's steps will typically be executed linearly in a sequential structure. As a result, many programs have a sequential structure in order to avoid writing complex code. However, sequential code requires a high level of skill from programmers because developing programming logic in a linear way can be difficult.

Example:

```
a = 6
print (a, "is a perfect number")
```

Output:

```
6 is a perfect number
```

In the previous example, the Python interpreter parsed the code line by line to produce an output.

Conditional Structure

The conditional structure is a well-known programming structure that is used to execute only a portion of the program while ignoring the remaining logical code based on the conditional statements.

Only partial statements are executed in a conditional structure, which allows Python interpreters to save time by not parsing the entire code.

If and if-else conditional structures are two well-known conditional branches used by Python programmers.

Looping Structure

Looping structures are useful when you want to repeat the same statement or programming logic in a program based on logical conclusions. The Python interpreter allows you to repeat a programming step until the condition is met.

To make the most of the looping structure, developers must write both loop starting and loop terminating logic. While and for loops are two common looping structures that Python programmers can use in their code.

If/Else Conditional Statements

To perform specific operations, conditional statements rely on fundamental decision-making. If the condition is not met, the conditional logic will skip that particular block.

Python includes a basic if/else statement for choosing between two blocks using a logical statement.

Syntax:

if condition:

execute statement

else:

execute statement

Program Code:

```
x = 31
if x % 4 == 0:
    print("This number is divisible by 4")
else:
        print("This number is not divisible by 4")
```

Output:

```
This number is not divisible by 4
```

Explanation:

- To begin, we must define a variable that will be used when we set up our condition for the if/else conditional.
- Indentation is required for the code that is eventually executed after the if (else) statement.
- Advanced programs use automatic input methods to get values from users.
- After storing the variable, the interpreter will parse the condition used by the if block.
- The Python interpreter will perform a remainder operation to see if the number is divisible by three.
- If it is divisible by three, the block immediately following the if statement should have been executed.
- Because the condition is false, the interpreter will skip the if block and instead execute the statements in the else block, which will result in the output.

Let's see an example of a condition that fulfills the if block.

Program Code:

```
x = 30
if x % 3 == 0:
    print("This number is divisible by 3")
else:
        print("This number is not divisible by 3")
```

Output:

```
This number is divisible by 3
```

If the condition is satisfied the print statement in the if block is executed, and the else block is skipped by the interpreter.

If Elif Else

Using multiple conditional expressions in a single program block allows you to make better use of conditionals.

Program Code:

```
n = 15
if n % 3 == 0:
        print("Number divisible by 3")
elif n % 4 == 0:
        print("Number divisible by 4")
else:
        print("Number not divisible by 3 and 4")
```

Output:

```
Number divisible by 3
```

In the previous example, the Python interpreter must check three conditions. When the Python interpreter determines that the first condition is true, it prints it and ignores the other two.

If any two statements are true, only the first one in the sequence of the code will be printed.

For Loops

Looping structures, like conditionals, are building blocks for Python software. Instead of constantly checking a condition, you can loop it using a for or while loop.

A for loop can be used with any data structure, including lists, tuples, and dictionaries.

Syntax:

> for i in object:
>
>> { Enter the body of a loop here }

When a condition is specified, the for loop can loop through all the items of the data structure.

Example:

```
v = [45,89,56]
out = 0
```

```
for val in v:
    out = out + val
print ("Sum of the 3 elements of the vector v:", out)
```

Output:

```
Sum of the 3 elements of the vector v: 190
```

In the previous example, instead of performing arithmetic operations on each element of the list, we simply used a for loop to automate this procedure.

While Loop

While the for loop is great for automating tasks, it can be difficult to write logical code since there is no way to apply a condition to the loop. This is where a while loop comes in handy.

A while loop will be provided prior to looping, with the condition being checked each time the loop occurs.

Syntax:

```
while condition
        {Enter the statement for a while loop here}
```

Example:

```
a = 0
b = 1
N = int(input("Enter number: "))
while b <= N:
    a = a + b
    b = b + 1
print ("The sum of numbers from 1 to", N, "is", a)
```

Output:

```
Enter number: 10
The sum of numbers from 1 to 10 is 55
```

Conditionals and loops can be nested to create more complex programs.

Break and Continue

Loops can complete a large amount of complex programming logic in a short period of time. While they are useful in many situations, they can consume a lot of run-time memory, causing programs to crash unexpectedly.

To solve this problem, Python provides two programming components known as break and continue.

Break Statement

When the Python interpreter encounters a 'break' in a program, it immediately ends the loop and moves on to the line following the loop. Any time the 'break' occurs inside a loop, the loop will end, and the next statements will be executed.

Syntax:

```
break
```

Example Program:

```
M = 10
j = 1
while j <= M:
    if j %2 == 0:
        print (j, "is divisible by 2 ")
    if j % 3 == 0:
        print (j, "is divisible by 3 ")
        break
    j = j + 1
```

Output:

```
2 is divided by 2
3 is divisible by 3
```

When the interpreter reads the break statement in the previous example, the program will end. What would the output be without the 'break'? (hint: all the numbers <= 10 that are divisible by 2 and 3...).

Continue Statement?

When the Python interpreter encounters 'continue' in a program, it immediately ends the loop and moves on to the next iteration. Keep in mind that this statement will not completely end the loop. Proceeding to the next logical statement in a loop will only save time and processing energy.

Example Program:

```
for letter in 'Productivity':
    if letter == 't':
        continue
    print('Letter now:', letter)
```

Output:

```
Letter now: P
Letter now: r
Letter now: o
Letter now: d
Letter now: u
Letter now: c
Letter now: i
Letter now: v
Letter now: i
Letter now: y
```

Exercises

1. Write a program that asks the user for an integer and calculates the factorial of the given number. Use a for loop to accomplish this task.

2. Write a program that counts the number of vowels (a, e, i, o, u) of a string given as input from the user. Loop the string and check if the current character is a vowel.

3. Create some code to produce a random number between 1 and 100. The program should then ask the user to guess the number and keep asking until the user has entered the correct number. Use a while loop to accomplish this task.

4. Write a program that prints the first n even numbers. Ask the user for the value of n. Use a for loop to generate the numbers, and an if statement to determine if the current number is even.

5. Write a program that prints the first n Fibonacci numbers. The Fibonacci sequence is a series of numbers in which each number is the sum of the two preceding ones. The first two numbers in the series are 0 and 1. Use a for loop to generate the numbers and break the loop when n numbers have been printed.

Chapter 8: Functions and Modules

Python supports a variety of programming paradigms. The functional programming paradigm is the most widely used programming paradigm for developers to write code in. Functional programming is adaptable and simple to use for simple projects that require fewer developers to complete the code. Because of the faster implementation of various programming components, the functional paradigm is also considered versatile.

Creating programs with functions may be difficult because you must always call the function within the program. With the help of a few examples, you can learn functional programming and create complex programs with less code.

A Real-World Example:

Functions were first used in mathematics to solve complex problems in discrete mathematics. Later, programmers began implementing this concept in order to reuse previously written code without rewriting it.

Let's use a simple mobile app to demonstrate how functions work in real-world applications.

Picsart is a popular mobile photo editing app that offers a variety of filters and tools for image manipulation. For example, the crop tool makes it simple for users to crop their images. Now, when Picsart developers write code, they typically use a variety of libraries, frameworks, and functions. Cropping, for example, necessitates its own function due to the numerous complex tasks involved in dividing pixels and providing output to the user.

Assume the developers wanted to update the application to include video cropping support. For programmers, there are currently two options.

1. They can design a cropping function from the ground up.
2. They can use the photo cropping function and add additional functionalities.

Many developers prefer option two because it is simpler and saves time. However, as previously stated, creating functions is not as simple. It requires a great deal of complex logic to connect the functions to the core application framework and other third-party libraries.

Types of Functions

System functions and user-defined functions are the two main types of functions.

The core Python library provides system functions, which are frequently used by developers to perform common tasks. 'print,' for example, is a system function that displays a literal string literal on the screen.

Developers, on the other hand, create user-defined functions specifically for their software. Users can also integrate third-party libraries' user-defined functions into their code.

Regardless of the type of code you use, keep in mind that the primary goal of using functions as a programmer is to solve problems with less reusable code.

How Do They Work?

The philosophy behind the use of functions in programming is similar to that of mathematical functions. The developer will first define a function with complex code logic and a name that can be called from anywhere in the program using unique programming components known as parameters. The developers then explicitly define what type of parameters the user can provide for fewer crashes.

If the function is not called, users will be unable to use the code logic that the developer created. Function calling is frequently displayed in the front end via buttons, tabs, and other graphical user interfaces. While it may be as simple as a tap for the end user, a function will be called programmatically in order for a software component to function properly.

How Should You Define Your Functions?

There is no need to define the default system functions because they are built. You can only call them. Even though programmers can modify system functions, doing so is not recommended because they are typically complex, and messing with them will break your code.

Python developers who want to create game-changing software, on the other hand, can use the "def" keyword to create functions.

A simple example is provided to help you understand function declaration in Python more quickly.

Program Code:

```
# Function to print a welcome message
def welcome():
    print ("Good morning, I Hope you are fine.")
welcome()
```

Output:

```
Good morning, I Hope you are fine.
```

Explanation:

- While this is a simple program, its workflow is similar to that of more complex programs. When working on real-world projects, the number of steps only increases.
- First, we use the 'def' keyword in line 1 to initialize a function in the program. If the def keyword is not used, the function will not work because the interpreter will not understand that it is a function.
- The name of the function is defined alongside def. The function is called "welcome" in this case. The same rules apply to naming functions as they do to variables.
- The body of the function is everything that comes after the comment. Variables, functions, and constants can all be part of a function body. The main core logic of the function is usually defined in this body.
- The body of the function is usually preceded by a comment or docstring. We used a comment in this example. When you use two single quotes to provide information about a function, this is referred to as a docstring.

If you are using multiple lines to provide information, then you can use three single quotes.

Example:

```
# This is an example of function that we are using for beginners
def myFunction():
    '''

    Author: John
    Function: myFunction
    What does it do? It simply prints
    '''

    print ("Hi! I wish you a wonderful day!")


myFunction()
```

The program's third line defines a print statement that display content on the screen. You can use as many built-in functions as you want in this area to make your program look more natural for the time being. Even though the data is static, it helps you understand how legacy applications work.

The final line shows how the developer invokes a function. In this case, myFunction() is a function call. There are no parameters between parentheses because this is a simple program. Multiple parameters can be used in complex programs. When the interpreter finds a function call, it immediately searches for the function and does whatever the function requests.

Function Parameters

There were no parameters in the previous example function. That is not the case in real-world applications, as programs are frequently complex and difficult to understand. To use functions, you must first create functions that use parameters and perform tasks.

Assume, based on the previous example, that we have two users for our application, and we need to greet them by calling them by their names.

Program Code:

```
def mysample():
# Function that prints the same welcome message to two different users
    print("Hi Sam, I hope you are fine!")
    print("Hi Tom, I hope you are fine!"")
mysample()
```

Output:

```
Hi Sam, I hope you are fine!
Hi Tom, I hope you are fine!"
```

To begin, create two print statements that use both input/conditionals and print statements to validate the user and display the correct output. This is overly complicated and unnecessary, as parameters can assist you in creating dynamic welcome messages for your users. Not just for two, but for thousands of users, with just a minor change when creating a function.

Consider this example function with a single parameter that can assist you in creating a dynamic message.

Program Code:

```
# This is an example function with a single parameter
def mysample(name):
    print ("Hi " + name + ". " + "How are you doing?")
mysample('Sam')
mysample('Tom')
mysample('John')
mysample('Mike')
```

Output:

```
Hi Sam. How are you doing?
```

```
Hi Tom. How are you doing?
Hi John. How are you doing?
Hi Mike. How are you doing?
```

Explanation:

- A function named 'mysample' is created, and the parameter 'name' is defined between parenthesis. Because the Python interpreter is intelligent enough to parse any data value provided by the user, you may not need to specify the data type for this parameter.
- The programmer used the arithmetic operator to divide the string after calling the parameter in the print function. As a result, whenever the user enters data, it is placed between the default strings.
- In the following lines, the developer has called the function with the parameter input. For complex applications, the parameter cannot be fixed and must be provided by the user. We used the default parameters in this example. The parameters provided by the developer are Sam, Tom, John, and Mike.

If you want to start creating more advanced functions, you can use Python's argument functionality.

Arguments of a Function

To fully utilize their capabilities, all modern applications use variables for the functions. In the previous example program, we used default arguments for the function parameter. However, for Python developers, always providing parameters by default is not ideal. Users can pass arguments to the function through all parameters. While there are several ways to pass arguments to function parameters, the most common are positional and keyword arguments.

Positional Arguments

When using positional arguments, programmers typically provide the values for the function parameters directly. It may appear to be perplexing, but many programmers use it since it is easier to implement. It is essential to remember the order in which positional arguments are passed.

Program Code:

```
def age(who, years):
    '''
    This function states the age of different people
    '''
    print(who, "is", years, "years old")

age('Mike', 35)
```

```
age('Tom', 24)
```

Output:

```
Mike is 35 years old
Tom is 24 years old
```

The arguments for the first instance in the previous example are 'Mike' and 35. Because no data types are specified, the Python interpreter will determine the value type and throw it to the function.

Parameter names are important because there is no direct way to understand the data type that we are using. A name is represented by a literal string, while a number is represented by an integer data type. A comma is typically used to separate all the arguments.

It is easy to make mistakes when using positional arguments, as demonstrated below.

Program Code:

```
def age(who, years):
    print(who, "is", years, "years old")

age(35, 'Mike')
age(24, 'Tom')
```

Output:

```
35 is Mike years old
24 is Tom years old
```

While the function produces an output, it is incorrect because the arguments are for opposite parameters.

Keyword Arguments can be used to define function parameters to solve these minor issues with positional arguments.

Keyword Arguments

With keyword arguments, you can directly pass arguments to the function parameter. Keyword arguments use parameter = value format to give arguments to any function.

Keyword Arguments cause less confusion but take more time to implement and hence are not often used by developers working on complex projects that involve a lot of code.

Program Code:

```
def age(who, years):
    print(who, "is", years, "years old")
```

```
age(who = 'Mike', years = 35)
age(years = 24, who = 'Tom')
```

Output:

```
Mike is 35 years old
Tom is 24 years old
```

The format in which keyword arguments are defined here is *parameter* = *argument*. In *who* = *'Mike'*, for example, *who* is the parameter and *Mike* is the argument.

Default Values

Not all values in a Python or other programming language program must be dynamic. Default values, also known as 'constants,' are sometimes used by developers when passing arguments to a function. Using default values for parameters is completely optional for programmers.

However, defining default values is recommended because it reduces boilerplate code and offers better data management if the project is complex. Boilerplate code is unnecessary, but it must be written by developers for the interpreter to function properly. While Python is clutter-free in comparison to other high-level languages, some changes to the code, such as defining default values, are required to improve code readability.

Program Code:

```
def age(who, years = 35):
    print(who, "is", years, "years old")

age('Mike')
age('Tom')
```

Output:

```
Mike is 35 years old
Tom is 35 years old
```

Because we have already defined a parameter value in the previous example, function calling becomes easier and takes less time.

It is important to remember that even if you have given the default value, the Python interpreter will end up replacing the argument if it is defined again.

Program Code:

```
def age(who, years = 35):
    print(who, "is", years, "years old")
```

```
age('Mike')
age('Tom', 24)
```

Output:

```
Mike is 35 years old
Tom is 24 years old
```

Despite the fact that the default value is 35, the argument for Tom is given as 5. In this case, the Python interpreter replaces it with the new argument value.

Scope

"Scope" is critical for developers to understand the various types of functions available and to find ways to use them without difficulty. Functions, like variables, have a local scope and a global scope, as previously explained.

Local scope variables are all variables created within a function that can only be used within it. By contrast, any variable that can be used is referred to as a global scope variable.

Remember that a function can have both local and global variables. As a result, all variables used in the function should be either local or global.

Why Is Scope Crucial?

The scope functionality is mostly used to maintain the garbage mechanism more effective. To increase the program's speed, all variables that have been replaced or have not been used in a long time are usually destroyed. While they can be recreated when the function is called, the process still consumes runtime.

Instead, when a variable with global scope is created, it will probably be called multiple times. Therefore , having a global scope is useful to avoid the need to reinitialize variables. Regardless of the software you are creating, using scope whenever possible can help you increase your efficiency while working on complex projects.

Local and Global Scope

Rule—1: Local Scope Variables Cannot Be Used in a Global Scope
Program Code:

```
def mysample():
    x = 12

mysample()
print(x)
```

Output:

```
NameError: name 'x' is not defined
```

The previous example declares a variable with the local scope and a value of 12. When we call the function and attempt to print the variable value from the global scope, we get a traceback error because local variables, unlike global variables, can only be called within a function.

Program Code:

```
def mysample():
    x = 12
    print(x)
mysample()
```

Output:

```
12
```

Because the function is called from the local scope, the program runs without error and prints the local variable to the computer screen using the print statement.

Rule—2: Regardless of their scope, all local functions can use all variables.
Program Code:

```
x = 23
def mysample():
    y = 45
    print(x)
mysample()
print(x)
# print(x) would produce an error
```

Output:

```
23
23
```

When the variable is called from the local and global scopes, the value of the variable 'x' is printed.

Rule—3: Local variables that are used by one function can't be used by another.
Program Code:

```
def f1():
    x = 12
    print(x)
f1()
```

```
def f2():
    print(x)
f2()
```

Output:

```
24
NameError: name 'x' is not defined
```

Because it is a variable from the local function, the print function works for the first time. The variable value, on the other hand, causes a traceback error for the second time because the function 'f2' can't access the variable of the function 'f1'.

It should be noted that variables in both the local and global scopes can have the same name without causing confusion. However, for better programming practice and to avoid confusion, it is recommended that local and global variables be given different names.

Modules

In a programming language, a module is a group of functions. You can use these groups of functions in any software component by simply importing the module and calling the function with your parameters as arguments.

Python imports modules much better than traditional languages like C and C++. Many programmers import modules in order to use the module's methods and add additional capabilities on top of it.

Syntax:

import { Name of the module }

Example:

```
import math
```

The syntax above will import all the built-in math module functions into your program. As a result, you can now present your arguments for these methods.

What is the function of Import?

Import is a Python library function that copies all the functions in a specific file and links them to the current file. In this way, you can use methods that aren't in the current file. Furthermore, creating modules is useful to avoid writing the same code over and over again.

How Do I Create Modules?

While importing modules from third-party libraries saves time, as a developer, you must be aware of the importance of creating modules on your own.

Assume you're developing a web application for a torrent service. It would be beneficial if you wrote a large number of functions to make the application work. To improve organization, it will be better to create a networking module and include all networking-related functions in it. Following that, you can create a module with a GUI and several functions to aid in the creation of a visually appealing application.

To begin creating a Python module, you must first create a text file with the.py extension. After you've created the.py file, you can now add all the functions to it. For example, in the.py module we just created, you could include the following function to multiply two numbers.

File – examplemodule.py

```
def sum(a,b):
# This method computes the sum of two numbers
c = a * b
return c
# The sum will be the output
```

We will show a sample script that imports the previous function as the module is created.

Program Code:

```
import examplemodule
```

After pressing the enter key, the functions in that module will be available to a Python programmer working on other projects.

Program Code:

```
examplemodule.sum(12,23)
```

Output:

```
35
```

The script will automatically detect the 'sum' function, and the sum will be displayed on the computer screen based on the arguments provided.

Modules and Built-In Functions

While creating complex and complicated software applications, developers can make use of several built-in functions and modules. While user-built functions are great for solving complex problems, they are difficult to implement and sometimes unnecessary because built-in functions can do the job.

1. print()

It is the most commonly used built-in function in Python. Everyone, from beginners to experienced programmers, uses the print() statement to display output on the computer screen. As previously stated, the content you want to display on the screen should be placed between the quotes.

2. abs()

It is a built-in function that returns the absolute value of any integer. If a negative integer is given as input, this function will return the positive value.

Program Code:

```
z = -65
print(abs(z))
```

Output:

```
65
```

3. round ()

It is a built-in mathematical function that returns the closest integer number to any given floating-point number.

Program Code:

```
x = 12.32
y = 4.23
print(round(x))
print(round(y))
```

Output:

```
12
4
```

4. max()

This built-in Python function that returns the highest number among a set of numbers. This function can be applied to any data type, including lists and variables.

Program Code:

```
x = 31
y = 78
z = 36
```

```
mymax = max(x,y,z)
print(mymax)
```

Output:

```
78
```

5. min()

This built-in function that returns the smallest number among a set of numbers.

Program Code:

```
x = 31
y = 78
z = 36
mymin = min(x,y,z)
print(mymin)
```

Output:

```
31
```

6. sorted()

It sorts all the elements in a list in either ascending or descending order, depending on your preference.

Program Code:

```
t = (5,857,165,43,430,60,753,15)
s = sorted(t)
print(s)
```

Output:

```
[5, 15, 43, 60, 165, 430, 753, 857]
```

7. sum()

sum() is a built-in function that takes as input a list or a tuple and adds their elements. All the elements of the list or tuple must have the same numerical data type. For example, if string data types are in the input, the program will fail with a type error.

Program Code:

```
t = (5,857,165,43,430,60,753,15)
s = sum(t)
print(s)
```

Output:

8. len()

This built-in function that returns the number of elements of the object in input.

Program Code:

```
t = (5,857,165,43,430,60,753,15)
s = len(t)
print(s)
```

Output:

```
8
```

9. type()

This function returns the data type of the object in input. If it is a function, the details about the parameters and arguments will be displayed as well.

Program Code:

```
t = 45.789
print(type(t))
```

Output:

```
<class 'float'>
```

String Functions

Strings are data types that require more attention from the programmer than other data types. Dozens of built-in functions in the Python core library have been created for programmers to make the most of data stored using strings.

1. strip()

It deletes the arguments passed to it as a parameter. The arguments will be removed from all instances where they appear.

Program Code:

```
text = "Python"
print(text.strip('hon'))
```

Output:

```
Pyt
```

2. replace()

It replaces one part of a string with another. If there are multiple words in the same string data type, you can specify how many to replace as a parameter.

Program Code:

```
text = "Have a great day!"
print(text.replace('great', 'wonderful'))
```

Output:

```
Have a wonderful day!
```

3. split()

It splits a string when the arguments you provided appear in the input text for the first time.

Program Code:

```
text = "There are three apples in the fridge"
print(text.split(' '))
```

Output:

```
['There', 'are', 'three', 'apples', 'in', 'the', 'fridge']
```

Since the argument we provided is a white space, in this case the output is a list with the words of the original string as elements.

4. join()

With this function you can insert a separator between the elements of a list, as long as they are characters.

Program Code:

```
country = ['Italy','France','Spain']
x = " ~ "
x = x.join(country)
print(x)
```

Output:

```
Italy ~ France ~ Spain
```

Exercises

1. Create a function that takes two numbers as parameters and returns the result of the sum of both numbers.

2. Create a function that takes a string as a parameter and returns the number of vowels in the string.

3. Create a function that takes two strings as parameters and returns a message indicating if both strings are equal or not.

4. Create a function that takes a number as a parameter and returns a message indicating if the number is positive, negative or zero.

5. Create a module with a function that takes a list as a parameter and returns the sum of all elements in the list. Import this module into another script and use the function to sum a list of numbers.

Chapter 9: Object Oriented Programming (OOP)

Until know we have discussed functional-oriented programming and provided several examples of code. While the functional programming paradigm is popular among independent developers, it can be difficult to implement when working with a team where many members must effectively communicate using their code.

Even though functional-oriented programming reduces a lot of code clutter, it is still difficult to import modules every time you create a new file. Importing more modules increases the program's run time exponentially.

Because of these issues, many programmers preferred to use Object-Oriented Programming languages such as Java during Python's initial release. But when Python 2 was released, everyone was enthusiastic to learn that Python had begun to support Object-Oriented Programming, transforming it into a multi-paradigm language.

With several examples, this chapter delves deeply into various object-oriented principles.

What Is OOP?

OOP is a popular programming paradigm in which classes and objects are used to organize functions into logical templates.

A class is a collection of data or methods that can be easily accessed using dot notation. Classes are accessible to variables and methods outside the class due to object behavior.

A Real-World Example:

Assume you are developing an application that explains details about various vehicles and models of those vehicles.

A functional programmer would create a function for each vehicle and then another for each model. It may appear simple when there are only a few vehicle models, but as the number of vehicle models grows, code reuse becomes difficult for developers.

In Object Oriented programming, however, the programmer will first create a 'vehicle' class and define various properties and values. The developer will then create a separate class for each type of vehicle. Because of the Object Oriented programming paradigm, the developer can access and call all those properties with a simple dot notation rather than creating functions for each property again.

Object Oriented programming saves time and is useful to reuse code thanks to features like polymorphism and inheritance.

How Do I Create Classes?

Classes are a way to create custom data types and they represent a blueprint from which objects are typically created. Classes include various logical entities such as attributes and methods. Specific rules must be followed when creating classes.

- All classes that are created must be preceded by the keyword 'class.'
- Variables created within a class are nothing more than class attributes.
- All attributes in a class are public and can be used at any time by using the . (dot) operator.

The syntax for class creation:

class ClassName:

Class-level attributes

Definition of the attributes

Initialization method

The self method that we'll discuss

Class methods

Specific methods (functions) of the class

In Python, you can't use reserved keywords for class names. Otherwise, a traceback error will occur, causing the application to crash.

How Do I Create Objects?

In Python programming, an object is an entity that has a state and behavior. Everything within a class can be considered an object. A variable created within a class, for example, can be used as an object. Objects are frequently used by programmers who are unaware of their existence.

What exactly is an object?

- Every object is made up of a state. A state usually reflects the properties of an object.

- Every object has a behavior. The behavior of an object changes depending on the method in which it is used.

- All objects have an identity. Objects use identity to interact with one another.

Assume there is a cat class that describes different cat features and their behavior. Objects in that class can be of various types.

- The name of the cat is typically used to identify the object

- Attributes such as cat age, type and color can be used to describe the state of an object.

- Behaviors of an object include jumping, sleeping, and running in relation to a cat.

How to create an object?

All you have to do to create an object is give it a name. For instance, if the 'Cat' class is defined, we can write:

Program Code:

```
obj = Cat()
```

This will generate an object called 'obj' belonging to the Cat class.

The Self Method

You should be aware of the self method, which is automatically created when a class is created.

The concept of a self method is similar to that of pointers in other programming languages such as C and C++.

If you want to call the methods, you must provide at least one argument to the self method. Every method that an object invokes is automatically transformed to a self object.

The __init__ Method

The __init__ method is similar to C++ and Java constructors. When a class is started, it runs as a default method. As a result, if you want to create an object with an initial value, you must enter those values into the __init method as a developer.

We'll make an example now by using self and the ___init__ method.

Program Code:

```
# Define a class called "Person" with the "name" attribute
```

```python
class Person:
    # Define a class attribute shared by all instances of the class
    species = "Homo sapiens"

    def __init__(self, name):
        # Initialize the name attribute as an instance attribute
        self.name = name

# Create two instances of the Person class with different names
person1 = Person("Alex")
person2 = Person("Sam")

# Print the names of each person
print("Name of person 1:", person1.name)
print("Name of person 2:", person2.name)
# Print the species attribute shared by all instances of the class
print("Species:", Person. species)
print(person1.name,'and',person2.name,'are',Person.species)
```

Output:

```
Name of person 1: Alice
Name of person 2: Bob
Species: Homo sapiens
Alice and Bob are Homo sapiens
```

In the previous example, we defined a class as well as instance attributes. There are few simple rules to keep in mind:

- You must provide a class name

- You must create at least one attribute

- You must provide a self argument and a __init__ method

- An object must be instantiated

- Following object instantiation, you can create instance attributes that can use the object.

lasses and Objects with Methods

In the previous example, a class attribute is created, followed by a method and the __init__ function. Finally, two objects are instantiated, and they are accessed using dot notation.

Program Code:

```python
class Person:
    species = "Homo sapiens"

    def __init__(self, name):
        self.name = name

    # Define a method to say hello
    def say_hello(self):
        return "Hello, my name is " + self.name

person1 = Person("Alex")
person2 = Person("Sam")

# Print the names of each person
print("Name of person 1:", person1.name)
print("Name of person 2:", person2.name)

# Call the say_hello method on each person
print(person1.say_hello())
print(person2.say_hello())
```

Output:

```
Name of person 1: Alex
Name of person 2: Sam
Hello, my name is Alex
Hello, my name is Sam
```

Explanation:

In the above example, a class attribute is created, and then a method is created along with the __init__ function. In the end, the object is instantiated, and the object is accessed by using the dot notation.

Inheritance

One of the most important aspects of Object-Oriented programming is inheritance. Inheritance refers to the process of defining a new class without adding new methods or arguments, but rather deriving them from other classes. The new class is commonly referred to as the child class. The parent class is the class from which all methods are inherited.

Real-World Example:

When developing real-world applications, inheritance comes in handy in a variety of situations. Assume you are developing a camera mobile application for iOS.

While creating the application, you may need to create several modules for the various functions it provides. You've noticed that you're reusing code for GUI interfaces after a few months of development because your team is still using function-oriented programming.

You decided to use an object-oriented framework for your project to save time and money. Since you're now using the OOP paradigm, you can reuse the code you've already written for GUI interfaces and link it to the new classes you're creating. This saves time and energy by allowing programmers to add new features without having to rewrite the old ones.

Syntax for Python inheritance:

class BaseClass:

{ Body of base class }

class DerivedClass(BaseClass):

{ Body of derived class }

Please keep in mind that both base and derived classes must follow all the previously described class rules.

Program Code:

```
# Define a base class "Polygon" with a method to return the number of
        edges
class Polygon:
    def __init__(self, num_edges):
        self.num_edges = num_edges

    def edges(self):
        return self.num_edges

# Define a subclass "Rectangle" based on the Polygon class
class Rectangle(Polygon):
    def __init__(self, length, width):
```

```python
        # Call the __init__ method of the parent class to initialize
        the number of edges
        Polygon.__init__(self, 4)
        self.length = length
        self.width = width


    # Define a method to calculate the area of the rectangle
    def area(self):
        return self.length * self.width

# Create an instance of the Rectangle class
rect = Rectangle(40, 10)

# Print the number of edges and the area of the rectangle
print("Number of edges:", rect.edges())
print("Area:", rect.area())
```

Output:

```
Number of edges: 4
Area: 50
```

Explanation:

In the previous example, we defined the class 'Polygon' first, and then built the second class 'Rectangle' on top of it. A rectangle with dimensions of 40 by 10 is created. When the 'area' method is called, the area of the square is computed. You can create another polygon class in the future by simply writing a method to calculate the area.

With enough knowledge of Object-Oriented Programming, you can create classes and objects that can interact in order to create software that uses many components and performs multiple tasks. Look at the open-source code hosted on GitHub to learn more about OOP.

Exercises

1. Create a class called Person with a constructor that takes in the person's name, age and occupation. The class should have methods get_name(), get_age() and get_occupation() that return the respective values. Create an instance of the class and call the methods to display the values.

2. Create a class called Student that inherits from Person. The class must have a constructor that takes in the name, age, occupation, and a list of subjects. The class should have a method get_subjects() that returns the list of subjects. Create an instance of the class and call the methods to display the values.

3. Create a class called Rectangle with a constructor that takes in the width and height. The class should have methods get_area() and get_perimeter() that return the area and perimeter of the rectangle, respectively. Create an instance of the class and call the methods to display the values.

4. Create a class called BankAccount with a constructor that takes in the owner's name, balance and type of account. The class should have methods get_balance(), deposit(amount) and withdraw(amount) that return the balance, deposit an amount, and withdraw an amount, respectively. Create an instance of the class and call the methods to display the values.

5. Create a class called Vehicle with a constructor that takes in the make, model and year. The class should have methods get_make(), get_model() and get_year() that return the respective values. Create two classes, Car and Truck, that inherit from Vehicle. The Car class should have an additional method get_type() that returns "Car" and the Truck class should have an additional method get_type() that returns "Truck". Create instances of both classes and call the methods to display the values.

Chapter 10: Files in Python

Python stores data in variables for both static and dynamic data. While variables are ideal for storing data during the execution of a program, they can be difficult to use when the data is sensitive and needs to be reused repeatedly. Variables can self-destruct in order to clear memory, which is inconvenient for users who want to save or reuse their data for multiple purposes. Python provides files to better interact with data of any size or format. Understanding file operations and implementing them in your programs is essential for creating better software as a Python programmer.

File Paths

Python programmers typically work with multiple files and two parameters. The first is the file name, which makes it easy to find, the second is the file path.

For example, if file.pdf is the name of a file, then "C:/ users/ downloads/file.pdf" is the path format of a file. The file extension in the file name 'file.pdf' is pdf. To manage files, most operating systems employ an efficient file management system.

It is critical to understand file management techniques. For this reason, you must understand the fundamentals of file managers used in the operating systems you are working in. For example, Windows use file explorer to manage files, whereas Mac systems use Finder. Regardless of the operating system and file manager you use, files are typically organized in a logical hierarchical order using root directories, folders, and subdirectories.

Hierarchical Arrangement of Files

For the program to detect the file location, you must enter the entire path. The entire path of the file is generally written hierarchically in order to determine the directory, subdirectories, and folders.

For example, in 'C:/users/sample/example.pdf,' C is the system's root directory, and sample and users are subdirectories within it. Because there may be multiple files with the same name in different folders, it is critical to use the entire path to determine the file's location.

As a programmer, you should be aware that Windows systems use Backslashes to differentiate between the root directory and subdirectories. Other operating systems, such as Mac and Linux, use forward slashes to distinguish between root and subdirectories.

If you don't want to use back or forward slashes while entering code on the terminal for whatever reason, you can use a function called os.path.join.

Program Code:

```
os.path.join('C', 'first', 'second')
```

Output:

```
'C\first\second'
```

Current Working Directory

While running complex code, you may need to interact with multiple files in the same directory as a Python programmer. A function called os.getcwd() can be used to help programmers interact with other files in the same directory. When your absolute path is identified, all files in the directory or subdirectory will be shown as output.

Creating New Folders

Several Python programs usually require users to generate files or the application to create files in different directories on its own. A save file for a game, for example, may be generated automatically by the software without any user intervention. All Python programmers must be aware of the importance of creating new folders for the applications they create. To create a new directory, use the os.makedirs() function.

Program Code:

```
import os
os.makedirs('D: /user/ Python/myfolder')
```

In the previous example, we first imported the 'os' module containing the system function design. The makedirs() function was then called with a path as the function parameter. "myfolder" is the name of the new folder created in the directory by the above function. You can check by opening your file manager or typing cd into a command prompt.

Please make sure to provide an absolute path to the directory where you want to create a new folder.

Functions to Manage Files

Files are complex and require a plethora of built-in functions to function properly. You can easily manipulate, open, and close files with Python from your IDE or terminal. By default, the Python interpreter can run both .txt and .py extension files.

If you want to work with file types like pdf and jpg, you'll need to install third-party libraries. By experienced Python programmers, these file types are referred to as binary file types.

To begin, we will create a file called example.txt on the path "D:/user/Python/example.txt" to help you understand the concepts of Files. You are free to use your path when creating a file.

This example txt file will be used to describe file functions such as open(), close(), write(), and read().

Assume the example.txt file contains the following:

Content:

```
This is a Python file.
```

How to Open Files

It is quite simple to open files with a Python command. All you need to know is the file's absolute path and how to use the open() function.

Program Code:

```
myfile = open ('D: /user / Python / example.txt ')
# This will open the file
```

The open() function, along with the parameter, is used in the example. The parameter in this example is the path provided to open a file. When a file is opened, the Python interpreter cannot read or write it, but the user can read it using the default viewer in which it was opened.

Before running this statement, make sure you have the necessary software to open the files. For example, if you try to open an.mp4 video file and there is not a native application that can open it, it will not be a viable solution.

What Happens?

When the interpreter locates the open() function, a new file object is created, and all changes made during this phase must be saved in order to be reflected in the original file. If the file is not saved, the Python interpreter will ignore all changes.

How to Read Files

When Python opens a file with the open() function, it creates a new object, and the Python interpreter can now easily read the entire file's content with the read() function.

Program Code:

```
filecontent = myfile.read()
# read() will scan all the content present in the file
```

Output:

```
This is a Python file.
```

In the previous example, we used the read() function to send the scanned data from the file to a new variable called 'filecontent.' Depending on the complexity of the file, you can also send the information into files to lists, tuples, or dictionaries.

While the read() function just prints the file content, the readlines() function can be used to organize the content of a file to new lines.

We will use a simple example to demonstrate this Python feature. First, in your working directory, create a new file called 'mynewfile.txt.' After opening the file, enter a few lines, as shown below.

mynewfile.txt:

```
This is an example of a document
We are simply connecting the dots
This information will be used to manipulate text
The Python interpreter is fast
```

Let's now call the readlines() function on the terminal.

Program Code:

```
myfile = open(mynewfile.txt)
# This variable helps us open a new file with the name provided
myfile.readlines()
```

Output:

```
['This is an example of a document \n', ' We are simply connecting the
dots \n', ' This information will be used to manipulate text  \n',
'Python interpreter is fast']
```

The output included a newline character \n for each line in the file. There are numerous advanced file functions that can be used when developing real-world applications.

How to Write Content to Files

You can use the write() function to insert new data into any file. The write() function is similar to the print() function, which is used by programmers to display content on the screen. It displays the contents of the file with the name you specify.

The open() function allows programmers to open the file in write mode. All you need to do is append an argument to let the interpreter know you want to open the file and add your own content.

Once you've finished writing into the file, use the close() method to close it and save it in its default location.

Program Code:

```
myfile = open('example.txt', 'w')
#This makes the file open in write mode
myfile.write ('This is how we write on files! \n')
myfile.close()
```

The output will show the content of the screen as well as the number of characters.

You can also append text as an argument by using 'a'.

Example:

```
myfile = open('example.txt', 'a')
# The file is open in write mode
example.write('This is a new version')
# The above statement will be added to the file provided
myfile.close()
```

To check whether the message has been appended, use the read function, as shown below.

```
myfile = read(example.txt)
print(myfile)
```

You can usually copy, paste, or cut files and folders using the default file manager functions, such as Windows Explorer and Mac finder. However, in Python you must use a built-in library known as shutil. It creates programming components that can be used to quickly copy, move, or delete files.

To use the shutil library's default functions, you must first import the library.

Chapter 11: Exception Handling

All applications occasionally crash as a result of incorrect user input or an error that occurs. It is possible to inform the user about why the application has crashed. If you can't help them, your software should at the very least detect that the application has collapsed and send the logs to your server to help them find solutions. Giving users a heads-up about errors is the bare minimum that modern application developers can do to improve their user experience.

Exception handling is a computer programming feature that helps developers to write scenarios for which an application may crash and explicitly instruct the user if this occurs.

Do you remember the famous "This application has stopped responding" with a red 'x' mark on Windows systems? It is one of the most well-known exception handling interfaces in any system. While your exceptions do not have to be of the highest quality, they should be adequate for a better end-user experience.

In Python development, writing valid exceptions is considered a sophisticated skill. Exception handling also assists programmers in detecting bugs and logical defects in a program early in the workflow. An exception also saves a significant amount of time during testing and maintenance.

Exception Handling Example:

- Go to your profile and try to tweet an image that is larger than 24MB. After loading, the Twitter web or app interface will display a popup informing you that your image cannot be uploaded due to its larger size.

- In this case, Twitter developers have built an exception handling interface to help users understand why their images are not being uploaded. Exception handling is an excellent tool for improving the user experience.

- All well-known third-party libraries include exception handling methods that you can import and use in your applications.

We will teach you how to handle exceptions using the Divide-by-zero error.

When you divide a number by zero, the value is usually undefined because it is referred to as an infinite value. Similarly, if a user of your application attempts to divide a number by zero, you must display a ZeroDivisionError. This error can be displayed using try and except statements.

'Try' and 'Except'

When creating exception handling tasks, you should be aware of the leading programming components try and except. The try block is where developers must specify the likelihood of finding the error in the Python interpreter. The except block, on the other hand, requires information about what to do if a specific error that we defined occurs during program execution.

Program Code:

```
# Try and except block in a function
def divide32(x):
    try:
        A = 32/x
        print(A)
    except ZeroDivisionError:
        print ("I can't divide by 0")


divide32(8)
divide32(0)
divide32(16)
```

Output:

```
4.0
I can't divide by 0
2.0
```

We started with a try and except block that told the interpreter where we could expect an error popup and what information should be displayed if there was one.

Different Types of Errors

Python documentation contains a plethora of system errors. When we discussed the Zero division error in the previous example, you may have noticed a straightforward approach. Different errors have different methods for avoiding them or running applications even when they are present.

Understanding the causes of some system errors can help you understand the fundamentals of debugging your applications.

Value errors

These errors occur when you pass arguments to a function that are not of the type that they accept. A value error can cause your application to crash unexpectedly.

Uploading a pdf file when only image files are permitted is an example of an exception trigger.

Import error

These errors occur when you are unable to import a module directly into your program. They are typically caused by a network connection failure or issues with online package managers.

Example of an Exception Trigger: You are unable to synchronize your data on your private cloud accounts due to an import error.

OS error

You may occasionally encounter issues because the software is incompatible with your operating system version. These errors frequently occur because the system kernel does not understand what the application is saying. These errors are fairly common when using Linux distributions.

Example of an Exception Trigger: The application crashes because the host is running an unsupported version of an operating system.

Type error

This error typically occurs when a user or developer enters a value for a data type that the application does not yet support.

Name error

When a variable or function that has not yet been defined in the program is called, this error occurs.

Index error

Index errors typically occur when you provide an index that is greater than the list you have created.

Chapter 12: Advanced Programming

Many third-party Python frameworks provide specific functionalities to programmers. It's sufficient to import the base libraries. That's why Python's popularity has skyrocketed. Libraries are great for developers to create real-world applications that ordinary users can use. You should be aware of certain commonly used Python libraries to write valid complex code without having to start from scratch.

The source codes for the majority of these libraries will be available for exploration on websites such as GitHub or Bitbucket.

Pip Package Manager

All operating systems make applications available to their users. Python isn't an operating system, but rather a software interpreter. Any software that is not written in Python can't run using a Python interpreter because the Python interpreter does not understand the source code used by that software.

There are thousands of paid and free Python software downloads available from many sources. A simple Google search for Python software for the domain you are interested in can provide thousands of results. To install this software on your own, you will need at least a basic understanding of executable files.

Python offers package managers to download package files into your operating system to be immediately executed. In this way, you can easily install the software you need. While there are many third-party Python package managers, the default pip is the most common and every Python programmer should be familiar with.

Why Using Pip

- New packages and dependencies can be installed.

- There is an index that lists all Python package repositories that are available on pip servers.

- Before installing the software, use it to go over the requirements.

- Remove all packages and dependencies that you no longer use.

First, check if pip is installed on your system. Pip is usually included with the Python.

Terminal Code:

```
$ pip —version
```

If it prints out the pip version information details, your system has the package manager installed. If not, you may need to manually download and install it from the official website.

How to Install Packages?

To install packages, you should always use the syntax format shown below.

> $ pip install name_of_the_software

For example, if you want to install the "Seaborn" package, the syntax is the following:

`$ pip install seaborn`

To check the information associated with the content before installing, use the command below:

`$ pip show seaborn`

This terminal code will return a lot of metadata information, including the Author, Package name and location.

Use the code syntax format below to uninstall any package installed on your system using the pip package manager.

Syntax:

> $ pip uninstall nameofthepackage

For example, to uninstall the Seaborn package you previously installed, use the command below:

`$ pip uninstall seaborn`

You can also search for a package using the code format shown below.

> $ pip search name_of_the_package

This will show you all packages from the package index for you to examine and select from.

Virtual Environment

Typically, when you install a package, you are also installing a number of dependencies. These dependencies may occasionally overlap with other software, causing the package to fail to install. To help developers in creating independent projects, the 'virtualenv' package can be used to create an isolated virtual environment.

First, use the pip package manager to install the 'virtualenv' package.

Installation command:

```
$ pip install virtualenv
```

Once the package is installed, you can use the below command to create a new directory using a virtual machine.

```
$ virtualenv mydir
```

All the packages, files, and software you install will be saved in this new directory, without interfering with any system dependencies or packages. To begin, run the following command to activate the virtual machine.

Terminal Command:

```
$ source mydir/bin/activate
```

After you've installed all of your packages, deactivate this virtual environment with the following command:

Terminal Command:

```
(mydir) $ deactivate
```

The sys Module

To master Python, it's crucial to understand how a Python interpreter works. An interpreter typically parses every variable, method or literal in the code before executing a logically written program and checking for syntax, type, and index errors. It is important to examine how an interpreter works and stores information required for the use of specific software.

The Sys module in Python makes it simple for developers to check this information.

```
import sys
```

path

This sys library argument will tell you the default path of the Python interpreter installed on your system:

```
print(sys.path)
```

argv

This method will return a list of all the existing modules in the system:

```
print(sys.argv)
```

copyright

This method will show the user the copyright information for the Python interpreter or software:

113

```
print(sys.copyright)
```

getrefcount

This method shows how frequently a program uses a variable or object:

```
print(sys.getrefcount(myvariable))
```

Unit Testing

Before developing, a programmer must ensure that the program follows all Python's guidelines. Even if the logic in your programs is correct, it may cause problems in the future due to practical issues. These bottleneck situations should be avoided in order to provide a better user experience.

Python allows and encourages programmers to check their code using unit testing frameworks. The framework 'unittest' is installed by default to force programmers to create testing conditions from scratch for their programs.

How Do Unit Tests Work?

You may become overwhelmed when testing their code because the Python documentation does not provide a specific set of rules for conducting unit tests. However, experienced programmers always emphasize that it is best to start testing code for methods first and then expand to other programming components.

- Using this methodology, you can test any part of the software.
- The tested code can be easily shared with other developers. Furthermore, eventual build and runtime errors during this process will be shared with your team.
- You can group tests and call them collections, and then manually organize them to keep these tests up to date.

Other third-party frameworks can be installed by programmers to improve their unit testing skills.

Scrapy

Scrapy is a Python library designed specifically for scraping purposes. Spiders are typically used to scrape data from dynamic websites and search engines. Scrapy is great to create advanced spiders capable of intuitively extracting data from web or mobile pages.

To install Scrapy, enter the following code into any package manager.

Installation command:

```
pip install scrapy
```

Requests

Requests is a Python library used to create HTTP requests for web or mobile applications. You can easily manage requests and responses for all web content that your application uses with Requests.

The web response data is typically in JSON format. t is normally difficult to read, but Requests parses the JSON file and displays the information in a readable manner. Scrappers also make use of the requests library to build automation software for major websites.

Use the default pip package to install Requests.

Installation command:

```
pip install requests
```

Pygame

Python is also used to create games for handheld consoles and mobile devices. Pygame is a popular third-party gaming framework among independent developers worldwide. Pygame includes both multimedia and physics libraries, allowing developers to create 2D and 3D games. Pygame also includes sound, mouse, keyboard, and accelerometer components for creating highly interactive games.

Most Pygame developers create games for Android phones and tablets because the SDL Pygame framework is highly adaptable to these devices.

Use the following command to install Pygame on your local system.

Installation command:

```
pip install pygame
```

Beautiful Soup

Beautiful Soup is a popular Python scraping library that can retrieve HTML and XML data from a variety of sources with a single click. It can generate an efficient parse tree of the various directories and sub-directories present on the website, allowing users to easily organize the scraped information.

Before scraping, Beautiful Soup understands the most recent technologies, such as HTML 5 elements on a web page. Beautiful Soup is used by several third-party software, including Ahrefs, to handle their premium keyword research tools, which frequently need to scrape data from billions of pages on the internet.

Use pip to install Beautiful Soup on your local system.

Installation command:

```
pip install beautifulsoup
```

Pillow

Pillow is one of many Python libraries that make image manipulation simple. Image enhancement is required in a variety of computer domains, and Pillow makes it possible by leveraging the legacy PIL project, which was considered a better image manipulation library written in C.

Pillow is a fork of the PIL project, which is no longer being developed. Pillow supports a variety of image formats, including png, jpeg, gif and ttf. Furthermore, you can use Pillow's built-in methods to perform many photo editing functions, like rotating, resizing, cropping, and changing filters.

Use pip to install the Pillow library on your local system.

Installation command:

```
pip install pillow
```

Tensorflow

Tensorflow is a well-known Machine Learning library for building advanced neural networks. Many developers also use Tensorflow within Deep Learning frameworks to develop software components that are frequently embedded in Deep Learning applications like facial recognition. Google created Tensorflow to make the development of complex machine learning models easier. However, it was later made open source so that enthusiastic developers could contribute to the project.

Tensorflow can be installed using any package manager, such as pip.

Installation command:

```
pip install tensorflow
```

Scikit learn

Scikit learn is a widely used machine learning model creation tool that is similar to TensorFlow. Many developers use it to create data analysis and analytics software. Scikit learn makes it simple for developers to incorporate advanced machine learning models into their code, such as clustering, Random forests, and K-means algorithms.

Scikit learn also supports complex neural networking algorithms used in scientific research, such as the development of genetic algorithms. To install it use the following command.

Installation command:

```
pip install sci-kit learn
```

Pandas

Data analysts are in love with Pandas because it is one of the most popular third-party libraries. While R is more popular among data analysts than Python, Pandas is still a good library for developers who want to create advanced data-analysis models. Pandas makes it simple to import and export huge amounts of data in a variety of formats, including SQL, JSON, and Excel. Furthermore, you can use Pandas with greater precision than other libraries for data cleaning and arrangement, which are high-level data analysis techniques.

Use package managers such as pip to install Pandas on your local system.

Installation command:

```
pip install pandas
```

Matplotlib

Matplotlib is a well-known Python library that is used in conjunction with Scipy to implement high-level mathematical functions in your code. Scipy and Matplotlib can be used together to create multidimensional arrays, which can then be used to write complex code to solve real-world scientific challenges. Many computer scientists rely on these libraries to keep their workflows running smoothly.

Matplotlib displays all acquired data in beautiful graphs to help you better understand the data flow. Tkinter is also used to logically arrange data. While Scipy focuses on scientific and technical computing, Matplotlib focuses on data visualization for enthusiasts and organizations.

Use pip to install Matplotlib on your local system.

Installation command:

```
pip install matplotlib
```

To use some of Matplotlib's advanced functions, make sure Scipy is installed using the command below.

Installation command:

```
pip install scipy
```

Twisted

Developers of web-based Python applications must be familiar with various networking concepts. While the core Python library provides enough resources and methods to write efficient networking code, it is always recommended that you use libraries such as Twisted to create complex code more easily. With a single click, Twisted implements networking protocols such as UDP, TCP, and HTTP. Twisted is the default networking component library for many websites, including Twitch.

Use pip to install Twisted.

Installation command:

```
pip install twisted
```

GitHub for Programmers

GitHub is useful for programmers because it allows them to collaborate with teams remotely. GitHub is based on a peer-to-peer GIT repository, so the changes of your code will be reflected in your teammates' computers as soon as they are connected to the internet.

GitHub provides two versions: free and professional. When you use the free version, your code is accessible to anyone who has a GitHub account. With the pro version, your code will be private, and only members of your team will be able to access it. Furthermore, all private repositories use advanced encryption algorithms to safeguard your data.

Why Is GitHub Essential for Python Programmers?

Regardless of the computer domain you work in, you may need to use third-party frameworks and libraries available on GitHub when creating projects. You can use GitHub or one of several third-party clients to instantly interact with local repositories.

Dependencies are used by GitHub and all Git-supported clients to easily sync libraries and modules into your code. The Git server's 'commit' option allows you to make changes to the code.

Use the Python shell to run the following command to create a new repository in your GIT server.

Installation command:

```
$ git config —global root "my project."
```

When you enter the git code into the console, a new project is created, and you can now create folders for your project. To start creating a directory on the root of your project, run the command below.

```
$ mkdir. ("Name of the repository: ")
```

If you don't know anything about the GIT server or project you're working on, type the following command into your console.

```
$ git status
```

In this way you are ready to begin developing your open-source project to help other programmers in your domain.

PART II

—

SQL for Beginners

Introduction

Welcome to "SQL for Beginners"! We will explore the powerful world of SQL (Structured Query Language) and relational databases, providing a comprehensive overview of the fundamentals, advanced techniques, and real-world applications of this essential data management tool.

The first section of this book will cover the basics of SQL and relational databases. We will start by introducing the concept of relational databases and how SQL is used to interact with them. We will then cover the basic syntax and commands of SQL, including creating and manipulating tables, inserting, updating and deleting data, and querying data using basic and advanced techniques. Throughout this section, we will provide practical examples to help the reader build a strong foundation in SQL.

In the second section of this book, we will explore more complex SQL techniques and optimization. We will cover topics such as joining tables, subqueries, grouping and aggregating data, and advanced filtering and sorting techniques. We will also delve into the use of stored procedures, functions, and indexing for performance optimization. This section will provide the reader with real-world applications and best practices to optimize their data management processes and improve the performance of their SQL queries.

In the final section of this book, we will focus on the integration of SQL with other technologies and applications. We will explore importing and exporting data to and from other formats, working with data in a distributed environment, building data pipelines, and automating data processes. We will also discuss the use of SQL in data analysis and business intelligence, and the security and privacy considerations that come with SQL data management. Throughout this section, we will provide practical applications and real-world examples, helping the reader to build the confidence and competence to effectively implement SQL in a wide range of data management contexts.

Whether you are a beginner to SQL or looking to expand your existing knowledge, this book will provide you with the essential skills and knowledge to effectively manage and analyze data using SQL. I encourage you to work through the practical examples provided in each section to reinforce your understanding of the concepts and techniques covered. I hope you enjoy reading "SQL for Beginners" and find it to be a valuable resource in your journey to becoming a proficient SQL user.

Chapter 1: Relational Databases and SQL

A relational database (RDB) is a structure that stores files in an organized way using rows, tables, and columns. In a relational database, information is often organized in one or more tables, and each table has a unique name.

The columns that comprise a table's structure determine the types of information that can be stored in that table. A row, also known as a record, is a collection of data items that correspond to a particular instance of an object described by the table. Rows are also referred to as records. Keys are unique values that identify a particular row in a database and are used to link that row to relevant data in another table.

The relationship between the tables is established through the use of keywords, which are the values that distinguish one row from another. The ability of relational databases to store and manage large amounts of structured data, their adaptability in dealing with different data types, and their assistance in maintaining data integrity have led to their widespread adoption. Relational database management systems (RDBMS) that are widely employed include MySQL, Microsoft SQL Server, Oracle, and PostgreSQL. Because of their exceptional suitability, relational databases are designed specifically for use with applications that require complex data links and transactions that involve multiple tables.

A relational database may, for example, contain multiple tables for customers, orders, and products in order to manage product inventory and track customer orders. Relationships between these tables may also be established to facilitate the management of product inventory and the tracking of customer orders.

Advantages of Relational Databases

The use of the relational database model for both data management and storage comes with a variety of benefits, including the following:

- Flexibility: It is simple to add new data, modify existing data, or remove data anytime it is required.
- Durability ensures that any changes made to the database will be retained indefinitely, even if the operating system becomes corrupted.
- For consistency, only information that satisfies the criteria set forth by the data validation rules may be added to the database.

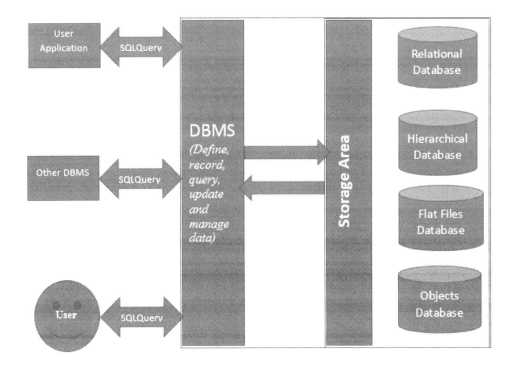

What is SQL?

The acronym SQL stands for Structured Query Language, which is used for maintaining and manipulating database systems. It may be used to conduct activities like building tables and indexes, adding, updating, and removing data, obtaining information from a database, and many other similar tasks. SQL is used in a wide variety of database systems, such as relational databases (such as MySQL, PostgreSQL, and Microsoft SQL Server) and NoSQL databases (such as MongoDB).SQL is a sequence of instructions, which means that you explain what it is that you want the database to do, and the DBMS is responsible for determining the most effective way to carry out your instructions. Because of this, you are free to concentrate on the logical aspects of the operations you perform on your database rather than the specifics of how to carry them out. SQL has existed for more than four decades, and despite its complexity, it continues to enjoy widespread adoption because of its adaptability, sturdiness, and ease of use. Learning SQL is a crucial ability that will help you deal with data more successfully, regardless of whether you are a software engineer, system admin, or data analyst. SQL is a structured query language.

Advantages of SQL

The abbreviation "SQL" refers to the "Structured Query Language," which is a language that may be used to manage and access relational databases. It offers several benefits that make it an appealing option. A few of the most important benefits include the following:

- Flexibility: SQL is a versatile phrase that can be utilized for a broad range of data-related activities, from basic data retrieval to complicated data processing and analysis. This range of jobs is made possible by SQL's ability to be used for various data-related tasks.
- Accessibility: SQL is a portable dialect used by many relational management systems due to its status as a standard. Because of this, SQL code may be moved from one relational database to the other, making it simple to transition between systems if this is required.
- Accessing data quickly and effectively SQL was developed to be a language that is both efficient and quick when it comes to retrieving data from relational databases. It contains many built-in functions and features that make obtaining, organizing, and analyzing data straightforward.
- SQL is a sophisticated and quite well language with a storied record of dependable performance. Its reliability stems from its lengthy history. Because of this, it is an excellent option for applications that are crucial to the operation of a company.
- Scalability: SQL can handle enormous databases that include millions of entries, so it is an excellent option for businesses that are required to store and retrieve massive volumes of data.
- SQL includes various security tools and features for preserving the integrity and secrecy of sensitive information, managing access to data and preventing unauthorized disclosure.
- When it comes to accessing and maintaining relational databases, utilizing SQL offers several benefits, some of which are listed below. SQL is a strong and adaptable language that may assist you in working with data more efficiently and successfully, regardless of whether you are a system administrator, a data analyst, or a software developer.

Chapter 1: Basic SQL Syntax and Commands

SQL allows users to communicate with databases using a set of fundamental instructions. The following are a few of the frequently used commands:

Create

The *Create* command is used to create different objects. One of the most important objects to store information is a database.

Syntax:

CREATE DATABASE database_name;

Code:

```
CREATE DATABASE office;
```

Output:

It results in creating a database named office in the system database folder.

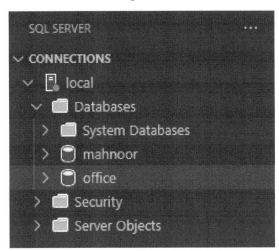

CREATE is also used to create tables within a database. The *Create Table* command creates the table and also specifies its columns and data types as follows:

Syntax:

CREATE TABLE table_name(column_name DATATYPE);

Code:

```
Create TABLE Employee_Tab(Name varchar(20), Age int, Salary int, Email
    varchar(30))
Create TABLE Customer_Tab(Name varchar(20), Age int, Email varchar(30))
Create TABLE Manager_Tab(Name varchar(20), Code int, Email varchar(30))
```

Output:

It creates a table named Employee_Tab, Customer_Tab and Manager_Tab in the Tables folder of the office database.

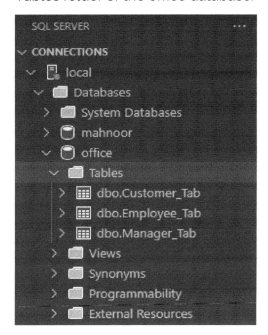

SELECT

SELECT will be the starting point for many queries because it tells the database which variables we want to see. We can either give the names of the columns, separated by commas, or use the * symbol, which will return all the columns in the table.

Syntax:

SELECT * FROM table_name;

Code:

```
SELECT * FROM Employee_Tab;
SELECT * FROM Customer_Tab;
```

Output:

	Name	Age	Salary	Email
1	John Doe	30	4000	johndoe@gmai...
2	Jane Doe	28	5000	janedow@gmai...
3	Jim Smith	35	5000	jimsith@gmail....

RESULTS

	Name	Age	Email
1	Janet Yew	20	janetyew@gma...
2	Peter Son	48	peterson@gma...
3	Andrew Smith	32	smith@gmail.c...

INSERT INTO

In SQL, data is inserted into a database using the INSERT INTO statement. In this case, the table name refers to the tag of the table into which you want to insert data. Column 1, column 2, column 3, etc., are the names of the individual columns of the table. The values value1, value2, and value3 correspond to the values you wish to enter into the corresponding columns, denoting them.

It is important to remember that you may insert many records into a table all at once if you use the same INSERT INTO command and add extra sets of information.

Syntax:

INSERT INTO table_name (column1, column2, column3, ...)

VALUES (value1, value2, value3, ...);

Code:

```
INSERT INTO Employee_Tab (Name, Age, Salary, Email)
VALUES ('John Doe', 30, 4000, 'johndoe@gmail.com'),
       ('Jane Doe', 28, 5000, 'janedow@gmail.com'),
       ('Jim Smith', 35, 5000,  'jimsith@gmail.com');
INSERT INTO Customer_Tab (Name, Age, Email)
VALUES ('Janet Yew', 20, 'janetyew@gmail.com'),
       ('Peter Son', 48, 'peterson@gmail.com'),
       ('Andrew Smith', 32, 'smith@gmail.com');
```

Output:

The output results in 3 rows are affected because we have entered three records in the Employee table.

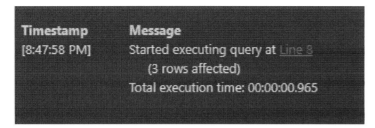

The output results in 3 rows are affected because we have entered three records in the Customer table.

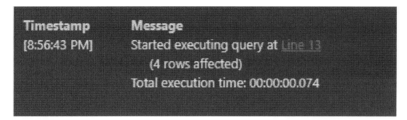

UPDATE

The UPDATE command in SQL changes the data already in a table.

The table name refers to the table title that this command will update. The SET clause allows you to specify the columns and values you wish to modify. The WHERE article governs which rows should be changed depending on the given conditions.

Because changing the wrong rows might result in inaccurate data, it is essential to utilize the WHERE clause with extreme caution. Before altering the data, it is recommended to validate your UPDATE statement using a SELECT query to validate the row that the change would impact.

Syntax:

UPDATE table_name

SET column1 = value1, column2 = value2

WHERE condition

Code:

```
UPDATE Employee_Tab
SET Name = 'Houston'
WHERE Salary = '4000'
```

Output:

Therefore, these results in the name John Doe are updated to Houston as his Salary was 4000 according to the condition mentioned.

	Name	Age	Salary	Email
1	Houston	30	4000	johndoe@gmai...
2	Jane Doe	28	5000	janedow@gmai...
3	Jim Smith	35	5000	jimsith@gmail....

DELETE

When you want to remove records already in a table, you may use the DELETE command in SQL.

Because accidentally removing the incorrect rows might result in lost data, it is essential to utilize the WHERE clause with extreme caution. Before removing the data, it is a good idea to validate your DELETE statement using a SELECT query to validate the rows the deletion could impact. This is a recommended best practice.

Be aware that the data you delete using DELETE statements is irretrievably destroyed and cannot be recovered under any circumstances. This information is gone forever. It is important to keep regular backups of your data to prevent it from being lost in the event it is inadvertently deleted.

Syntax:

DELETE FROM table_name

WHERE condition

Code:

```
DELETE FROM Customer_Tab
WHERE Name = 'Peter Son';
DELETE FROM Employee_Tab
WHERE Name = 'Jim Smith';
DELETE FROM Customer_Tab
WHERE Age = '32';
```

Output:

	Name	Age	Email
1	Janet Yew	20	janetyew@gma...
2	Andrew Smith	32	smith@gmail.c...

RESULTS

	Name	Age	Salary	Email
1	Houston	30	4000	johndoe@gmai...
2	Jane Doe	28	5000	janedow@gmai...

RESULTS

	Name	Age	Email
1	Janet Yew	20	janetyew@gma...
2	Janet Yew	20	janetyew@gma...
3	James Clark	23	clark@gmail.com

DROP

It is used to remove the table's structure and any entries. You must use the DROP statement with extreme care since it will irreversibly erase the object you provide together with all its contents. The data that has been destroyed cannot be retrieved once the DROP instruction has been carried out.

The DROP command may be used to destroy additional database objects and tables. Some examples of these other database objects are indexes, views, and databases. There may be particular subtle modifications in the syntax of these objects, but the fundamental idea remains the same.

Syntax:

DROP TABLE table_name;

Code:

```
DROP TABLE Manager_Tab;
```

Output:

It results in dropping a table named Manager_Tab from the table's folder.

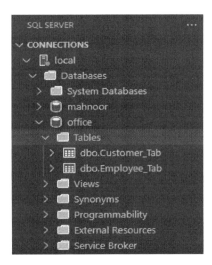

SELECT FROM

In contrast to the column names, we want the database to get, we are also required to provide the table from which the columns should be retrieved. To do this, we will type the term FROM, then the table's name.

Syntax:

SELECT column1, column2

FROM table_name;

Code:

```
SELECT Name, Age FROM Employee_Tab;
SELECT Age, Email FROM Customer_Tab;
```

Output:

Here only the Name and Age columns have been selected from Employee Table.

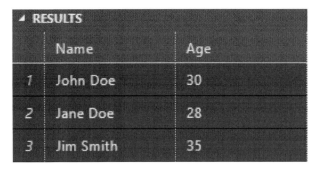

Here only the Age and Email columns have been selected from Customer Table.

	Age	Email
1	20	janetyew@gma...
2	48	peterson@gma...
3	32	smith@gmail.c...

These are just a few of the fundamental SQL commands available. Extra commands and syntax may need to be learned, but this will depend on the DBMS. It is vital to solidly accept these fundamental instructions to interact with a system successfully.

Chapter 2: SQL Data Types

Basic SQL Syntax

The Structured Query Language, or SQL, comprises several fundamental principles and grammar used while composing SQL queries. The following are a few of the often-observed syntaxes:

- Although SQL keywords do not care about capitalization, it is best practice to write them with all capital letters.
- The semicolon is required after SQL statements (;).
- In SQL, the keywords are almost always typed with an uppercase letter.
- String values are required to be encapsulated in single quotation characters (').
- Executing SQL instructions is impossible until the semicolon has been reached.
- SQL statements rely on the lines of text they are written on. We can utilize a single SQL query on more than one text line if necessary.
- SQL queries are processed starting at the left and working to the right.
- It is not necessary to put numerical numbers in quotation marks.
- SQL comments are denoted by a pair of hyphens (--) at the opening of the line and continue to the decision.
- You can carry out most of the tasks in a database using SQL statements.
- Structured Query Language relies on Tuple Relationship Calculus and Relational Algebra.

Data Types

A data type in SQL Server specifies the information that may be found in a database column or variable. In the process of creating a table, this phase is required and very necessary. Inappropriate data types in a table may contribute to various problems, including ineffective query optimization, poor performance, and truncated data.

- Data types that deal with numbers are called Numeric, such as INT, TINYINT, BIGINT, FLOAT, and REAL, amongst others.
- Date and time-related data types include dates, TIME, and DATETIME, among others.
- Data types for characters and strings include the likes CHAR, VARCHAR, and TEXT.
- Data types that correspond to Unicode character strings, such as NCHAR, NVARCHAR, and NTEXT, among others.
- Binary data types include things like BINARY and VARBINARY, amongst others.

- Miscellaneous data types include CLOB, BLOB, XML, CURSOR, and TABLE.

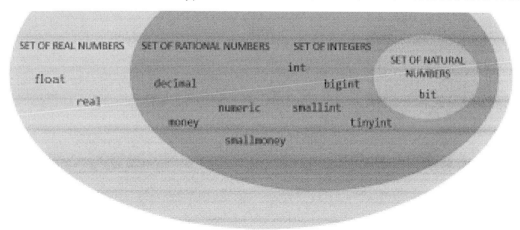

SQL is equipped with several fundamental data types that may be used to save various kinds of information in a database. These are the details of the data type as mentioned above

INT

INT stands for "integer" and is the data type used to hold entire numbers and integers. The size of an INT may vary depending on the particular SQL implementation, although it generally falls between the range of -2147483648 and 21473647.

Syntax:

variable_name INT

Code:

```
CREATE TABLE Employee_Tab
(
    Age INT
);
```

BIGINT

BIGINT is a whole integer data type that may be used to store bigger integer values. BIGINT values normally fall in the range of -9223372036854775808 to 9223372036854775807; however, the size of a BIGINT might vary depending on the particular SQL implementation.

Syntax:

variable_name BIGINT

Code:

```
CREATE TABLE Employee_Tab
```

```
(
    Salary BIGINT
);
```

DECIMAL

The DECIMAL data type for decimal numbers is used to hold numbers with a decimal point that is always the same. Depending on the SQL implementation, the length of a DECIMAL may vary anywhere from -1038+1 to 1038-1, although, in general, it falls somewhere in that region.

Syntax:

variable_name DECIMAL

Code:

```
CREATE TABLE Manager_Tab
(
    Income DECIMAL,
);
```

FLOAT

FLOAT is a floating-point number data type that is used for the storage of values that have a fractional component. A FLOAT's size may vary according to the particular SQL implementation, although it is more often than not in the range of -1.79E+308 to 1.79E+308.

Syntax:

variable_name FLOAT

Code:

```
CREATE TABLE Manager_Tab
(
    Average_Salary FLOAT
);
```

DOUBLE

DOUBLE is a floating-point number data type that stores bigger values that include a fractional component. The type is called DOUBLE. A DOUBLE's length varies according to the particular SQL implementation; however, the range for this value is normally between -2.23E+308 and 2.23E+308.

Syntax:

variable_name DOUBLE

Code:

```
CREATE TABLE Manager_Tab
(
    Yearly_Allounce DOUBLE
);
```

CHAR

CHAR is a string data type with a predetermined length used to store character strings. The size of a CHAR is measured in characters and has a variable limit that may fall between 0 and 255.

Syntax:

variable_name CHAR(char_length)

Code:

```
CREATE TABLE Customer_Tab
(
    Email CHAR(30)
);
```

VARCHAR

It is a variable-length string data type used to hold character strings. VARCHAR stands for "variable character." The length of a VARCHAR is measured in characters and has a width that may be anything from 0 to 65535 characters long.

Syntax:

variable_name VARCHAR(varchar_length)

Code:

```
CREATE TABLE Customer_Tab
 (
    Name VARCHAR(20)
);
```

TEXT

TEXT is a data type that can hold a variable number of bytes of text and has a string length that may vary. A TEXT's size may vary according to the particular SQL implementation, although the range of possible values is normally between 0 and 231 -1 character.

Syntax:

variable_name TEXT

Code:

```
CREATE TABLE Order_Tab
(
   Order_Details TEXT
);
```

DATE

DATE is a data type for dates that can store dates in the format of YYYY-MM-DD. You may save dates using this type.

Syntax:

variable_name DATE

Code:

```
CREATE TABLE Order_Tab
(
   Order_date DATE
);
```

TIME

TIME is a data type for times that are stored in HH:MM: SS.

Syntax:

variable_name TIME

Code:

```
CREATE TABLE Order_Tab
(
   Order_time TIME
);
```

Chapter 3: SQL Data Structures

Databases are organized to provide straightforward access, administration, and modification of the data sets they contain.

They are used by businesses to track all operations, get insight into what will help them function more effectively, and, consequently, assist ownership, managers, and analysts in making better choices.

The term "data structure" refers to the many methods of preserving data on a machine and is a vital component of the style of any central database. The operations that may be performed on these data structures and the instructions given to them to execute them are called algorithms. It is common for the fundamental functions of algorithms to be adapted specifically to the structure of the data structure.

How to Use Data Structures

In addition to enabling Core OS functions and resources and storing newly produced data for data permanence, data structures also store newly created data. Linked lists, trees, and queues are three different data structures that may handle memory allocation, file directories' administration, and processes' scheduling. Packets may be shared by developers using the TCP/IP protocols that are arranged using data structures. For binary search trees, for instance, there are various techniques for efficient ordering and sorting, and priority queues make it possible for programmers to handle objects while adhering to a predetermined order of priority.

Various straightforward methods are available for indexing and searching your data inside the various data structures. In large data applications, data structures also play an important role in ensuring high performance and scalability, which is why these applications are so important.

How to Select Data Structures

A variety of factors may aid the categorization of data structures. For instance, they may have a linear structure, similar to an array, in which the data items occur in a specific sequence. They may have a nonlinear structure like a graph, where the components are not arranged in any particular order.

Homogeneous data structures demand that all components have the same data type, but heterogeneous data structures can store data of various sorts. In contrast, data structures may either be static, in which the sizes and ram locations are predetermined, or dynamic, in which the sizes and storage locations are adjustable according to the requirements of the task at hand.

There is no simple solution to the question of which data structure you can implement. Each data format might have advantages and disadvantages, depending on the use-case situation. As a result, it is essential to consider the operations that you would execute on the data before making a choice about which to utilize.

For example, although retrieving any member of an array using the array's index is simple, linked lists are preferable when you want to resize the items in the array. On the other side, if you use a data structure that is neither appropriate, the duration of your program's execution will be increased, and the program will not respond properly.

When selecting a data structure, developers often take into consideration the following five factors:

- The kind of information you want to save is called the Data Type.
- Use Case refers to how you intend to put the knowledge to use.
- Location refers to the place where the data are kept.
- The most effective method for you to arrange things so that it is simple to reach is efficiency.
- How to use your storage reserve and maximize its potential

Stack Data Structure

There are several motivations for putting a stack into action on a SQL server. Stacks eliminate RAM, which is beneficial in a front-end crash. You may use them to keep an audit trail, allowing you to examine a log if anything goes wrong.

LIFO and FIFO are the two possible ordering methods for stacked items. A FIFO stack, also known as a First In, First Out stack, may be managed from either end, meaning that items can be attached to or eliminated from either the front or the rear of the stack. Conversely, a LIFO stack, which stands for "last in, first out," can only be operated from one end.

Popping refers to the process of removing an object from a stack, whereas pushing refers to the process of introducing an element to the stack. Learning these words is beneficial because of how often they are used. If you want to eliminate an entry from the stack, you may do so by deleting the row that has the stack order value that is highest as follows

Code:

```
CREATE TABLE Stack_Tab
  (
```

```
  id INT PRIMARY KEY,
  stack_value INT,
  stack_order INT,
);
Select * FROM Stack_Tab
DELETE FROM Stack_Tab
WHERE stack_order = (SELECT MAX(stack_order) FROM Stack_Tab);
```

Output:

Tree Data Structure

Items are organized in a hierarchical fashion inside trees. In a tree structure, every node is connected to a child node, a parent node, or both. The nodes each have a key value connected with them, and they all branch off of a single simple node in the tree.

The SQL tree structure is handy when storing data in a database with numerous levels since it allows you to organize it hierarchically. They avoid the hassle of doing several searches for each node to reach its child node, which is a huge time saver.

In addition to this, they assist us in retrieving all of the data by constructing the structure in the code.

Binary trees are a popular sort of tree that may be found. They are used rather commonly in search applications as well as expression solvers. In a binary tree, each node may only have a maximum of two child nodes at a time.

Code:
```
CREATE TABLE Tree_Tab
 (
  tree_id INT PRIMARY KEY,
  p_id INT,
  tree_value VARCHAR(100),
  FOREIGN KEY (p_id) REFERENCES Tree_Tab(tree_id)
);
SELECT * FROM Tree_Tab
```

Output:

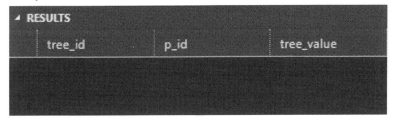

Linked List Data Structure

Linked lists are sequential data structures connected to one another in a linear direction. It is therefore impossible to retrieve a linked list in a random order. Sequential access is the only option. The elements of a linked list are called "nodes." Each node has a key and a pointer that directs to the next node. "Head" and "Tail" refer to the nodes located at the beginning and at the end of a linked list. There are three different classifications for linked lists:

- Singly Linked List: When using these linked lists, the only direction of navigation available is forward.
- Doubly Linked List: In the case of doubly linked lists, it is possible to navigate either forward or backwards across the list. This is accomplished by the use of an extra pointer that is referred to as the prior.
- Circular Linked Lists: In this particular instance, the Tail's next pointer is linked to the Head, and the prior pointer of the noggin is linked to the Tail of the list.

A linked list can have the following operations carried out on it.

- Search: Pressing the key k will allow you to locate the first element, and you may return the reference to this element.
- Insert: You can insert items at the start of the gradient, at the termination of the linked list, or anywhere in the center of the list.
- Delete: Similarly, and you have the option of removing items from the Head of the queue, the middle of the list, or the end of the list.

Code:

```
CREATE TABLE Linked_List_Tab
(
  LL_id INT PRIMARY KEY,
  next_LL_id INT,
  FOREIGN KEY (next_LL_id) REFERENCES Linked_List_Tab(LL_id)
);
Select * FROM Linked_List_Tab
```

Output:

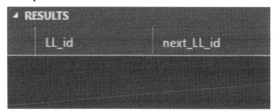

Chapter 4: Working with Tables

Creating Tables

Creating new tables in a database is possible using the create command. All required to make a table is to issue a "create tables" command, which allows you to define the table's columns and associated data types.

Syntax:

CREATE TABLE table_name(column_name DATATYPE);

Code:

```
Create TABLE Store_Tab(Store_Name varchar(20), Store_id int,
        Store_Location varchar(50))
Create TABLE Staff_Tab(Staff_Name varchar(20), Staff_id int,
        Staff_salary BIGINT)
```

Output:

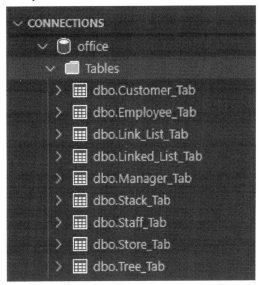

Altering Tables

The ALTER TABLE command in SQL is used to change the format of a preexisting table in a database.

Syntax:

ALTER TABLE table_name [Alteration Used]

Code:

```
ALTER TABLE Staff_Tab ADD Staff_email varchar(40);
SELECT * FROM Staff_Tab
ALTER TABLE Store_Tab DROP COLUMN Store_Location;
Select * FROM Store_Tab
```

Output:

Deleting Tables

When you want to remove records already in a table, you may use the DELETE command in SQL.

Syntax:

DELETE FROM table_name

WHERE condition

Code:

```
DELETE FROM Customer_Tab
WHERE Name = 'Peter Son';
```

Output:

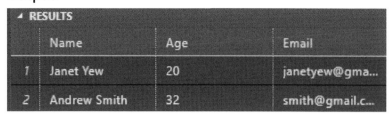

Inserting Data

In SQL, entering data into the database is achieved with the help of the INSERT INTO command. The table name in this context refers to the table title into which you want to put data. The names of the different columns included in the table are given in the form of their column numbers, such as column 1, column 2, column 3, etc. The values value1, value2, and value3 relate to the values you want to put into the respective columns, indicating them. Those values may be found in the respective columns.

Syntax:

INSERT INTO table_name (column1, column2, column3, ...)

VALUES (value1, value2, value3, ...);

Code:

```
INSERT INTO Store_Tab (Store_Name, Store_id )
VALUES ('Printer Store', 30),
       ('Grocery Store', 22)
Select * from Store_Tab
INSERT INTO Staff_Tab (Staff_Name , Staff_id, Staff_salary,Staff_email)
VALUES ('Janet Yew', 20, 5000),
       ('Peter Son', 48, 60000),
       ('Andrew Smith', 32, 2500);
Select * from Staff_Tab
```

Output:

◢ RESULTS

	Store_Name	Store_id
1	Printer Store	30
2	Grocery Store	22

◢ RESULTS

	Staff_Name	Staff_id	Staff_salary
1	Janet Yew	20	5000
2	Peter Son	48	60000
3	Andrew Smith	32	2500

Updating Table

In SQL, the UPDATE command is executed whenever a need exists to modify the data already stored in a database.

Syntax:

UPDATE table_name

SET column1 = value1, column2 = value2

WHERE condition

Code:

```
UPDATE Staff_Tab
SET Staff_id = '35'
WHERE Staff_Name = 'Andrew Smith'
Select * from Staff_Tab
```

Output:

	Staff_Name	Staff_id	Staff_salary
1	Janet Yew	20	5000
2	Peter Son	48	60000
3	Andrew Smith	35	2500

Deleting Data

You can employ the DELETE command in SQL to delete

records from a table if you already have entries in the table and wish to remove them.

Syntax:

DELETE FROM table_name

WHERE condition

Code:

```
DELETE FROM Staff_Tab
WHERE Staff_Name = 'Peter Son';
Select * from Staff_Tab
```

Output:

	Staff_Name	Staff_id	Staff_salary
1	Janet Yew	20	5000
2	Andrew Smith	35	2500

RESULTS

Chapter 5: Basic and Advanced Query Techniques

Structured Query Language, or SQL for short, is a language that facilitates communication with relational databases. The following is a list of some fundamental and sophisticated methods for choosing data in SQL:

JOIN

The JOIN operation combines the data from two or more tables, given that there is at least one common column between them.

Syntax:

SELECT * FROM table1

JOIN table2

ON table1.column1 = table2.column2

Code:

```
SELECT *
FROM Store_Tab
JOIN Staff_Tab
ON Store_Tab.Store_id = Staff_Tab.Staff_id;
```

Output:

Store_Name	Store_id	Staff_Name	Staff_id	Staff_salary	Staff_email

GROUP BY

This function groups data according to your column and produces aggregate statistics such as SUM, AVG, MIN, MAX, etc.

Syntax:

Select column_name , SUM(column_name)

From table_name GROUP BY column_name

Code:

```
SELECT Store_id, SUM(Store_id)
FROM Store_Tab
GROUP BY Store_id;
```

Output:

	Store_id	(No column na...
1	22	22
2	30	30

RESULTS

HAVING

The HAVING clause is a filter that sorts groups according to a certain condition.

Syntax:

Select column_name , SUM(column_name)

From table_name Group By column_name

Having SUM(column_name) [Condition]

Code:

```
SELECT Store_id, SUM(Store_id)
FROM Store_Tab
GROUP BY Store_id
HAVING SUM(Store_id) > 10;
```

Output:

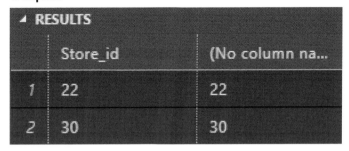

	Store_id	(No column na...
1	22	22
2	30	30

RESULTS

UNION

The UNION operator combines the findings of many SELECT queries into a single overall set of findings.

Syntax:

SELECT column_name FROM table_name UNION SELECT column_name FROM table_name

Code:

```
SELECT Store_Name
FROM Store_Tab
UNION
SELECT Staff_Name
FROM Staff_Tab;
```

Output:

	Store_Name
1	Andrew Smith
2	Grocery Store
3	Janet Yew
4	Printer Store

ORDER BY

We can sort the output of a query in SQL by using the "ORDER BY" clause, which allows you to sort the results in either descending or ascending order. When sorting the results of the SELECT mainly depending on one or even more columns, the "ORDER BY" phrase is utilized in the statement.

Syntax:

Select column 1, column 2

From table_name

Order column_name

Code:

```
SELECT Store_Name,Store_id
FROM Store_Tab
ORDER BY Store_id
```

Output:

	Store_Name	Store_id
1	Grocery Store	22
2	Printer Store	30

RESULTS

ORDER BY DESC

It is possible to categorize the outcome set in ascending or descending directives using the ORDER BY command.

The ORDER BY command will default sort the result set using an ascending sorting order. Use the DESC keyword to sort the entries in descending order from highest to lowest.

Syntax:

Select column 1, column 2

From table_name

Order column_name DESC

Code:

```
SELECT Staff_Name, Staff_salary, Staff_id
FROM Staff_Tab
ORDER BY Staff_id DESC;
```

Output:

	Staff_Name	Staff_salary	Staff_id
1	Andrew Smith	2500	35
2	Janet Yew	5000	20

RESULTS

ORDER BY Ascending example:

Syntax:

Select column 1, column 2

From table_name

Order column_name ASC

Code:
```
SELECT Staff_Name,Staff_salary,Staff_id
FROM Staff_Tab
ORDER BY Staff_id ASC;
```

Output:

	Staff_Name	Staff_salary	Staff_id
1	Janet Yew	5000	20
2	Andrew Smith	2500	35

INTERSECT

The UNION command and the INTERSECT operator work on a single set of SQL statements, whereas the INTERSECT operator acts on two statements. The INTERSECT and UNION operators function as OR operators. However, the INTERSECT operator also functions as an AND operator. This is the chief difference between the two.

Syntax:

SELECT column_name FROM table_name

Intersect

SELECT column_name FROM table_name

Code:
```
SELECT Store_id FROM Store_Tab
INTERSECT
SELECT Staff_id FROM Staff_Tab;
```

Output:

	Store_id
1	20

MINUS

The MINUS command also works on two different SQL queries simultaneously. The MINUS command begins by retaining the result from the first statement. It then takes the result received from the second statement and subtracts it from the result

151

acquired from the first statement to arrive at the final result. If the second statement produces outcomes that were not obtained from the first statement, then the first result will be disregarded, and the second result will be considered valid. It is important to notice that the MINUS command may only choose values unique from one another.

Syntax:

SELECT column_name FROM table_name

MINUS

SELECT column_name FROM table_name

Code:

```
SELECT Store_id FROM Store_Tab
MINUS
SELECT Staff_id FROM Staff_Tab;
```

Output:

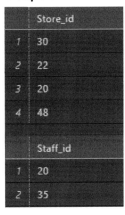

	Store_id
1	30
2	22
3	20
4	48

	Staff_id
1	20
2	35

Chapter 6: Advanced SQL Techniques and Optimization

Joining Tables and Working with Multiple Data Sources

In many scenarios, it can be challenging to work with data that is spread across multiple tables or data sources. This is where the concept of joining tables comes into play. Joining tables is the process of combining data from numerous tables into a single result set. This is achieved by identifying a common column between the tables that can be used to match the rows. By doing so, we can create a more comprehensive and useful dataset that can provide valuable insights and aid in decision-making.

Joining tables in SQL is a fundamental technique that is widely used in data management and analysis. It allows us to retrieve data from different tables and combine it into a single result set. Joining tables are performed using the JOIN operator, which can be used with different types of joins, such as inner joins, left outer joins, and right outer joins. The type of join used depends on the desired result.

Inner joins are the most popular type of join used in SQL. They retrieve only the rows that have matching values in both tables. This means that if there are no matching rows, they will not be included in the result set. In contrast, left and right outer joins retrieve all rows from one table and matching rows from the other table. If there are no matching rows, the non-matching rows will be filled with NULL values. This can be useful in situations where we want to retrieve all the data from one table and only the matching data from the other table.

Joining tables in SQL can be a complex process, especially when dealing with large datasets. It requires careful planning and consideration of the data structure and relationships between the tables. However, once mastered, it can be a powerful tool for data analysis and management. By merging data from multiple sources, we can gain a more comprehensive understanding of our data and make more enlightened decisions based on the insights gained.

In conclusion, joining tables is an essential technique in SQL for working with data that is spread across multiple tables or data sources. It allows us to combine data from different tables into a single result set, providing us with more comprehensive and useful data for analysis and decision-making. By using different types of joins, we can retrieve the desired data and gain valuable insights into our data. While it can be complex, mastering this technique can greatly improve our ability to manage and analyze large and complex datasets.

Joining tables is an essential skill for anyone who works with relational databases, and it is used extensively in data analysis, reporting, and other data management tasks.

INNER JOIN

The INNER JOIN keyword returns only the rows where there is a match in both tables based on the specified join condition.

Syntax:

SELECT *

FROM table1

INNER JOIN table2

ON table1.column = table2.column;

LEFT OUTER JOIN

LEFT OUTER JOIN returns all left table rows and matching right table rows. The right table's columns will be NULL if there is no match.

Syntax:

SELECT *

FROM table1

LEFT OUTER JOIN table2

ON table1.column = table2.column;

RIGHT OUTER JOIN

The RIGHT OUTER JOIN keyword returns all right table rows and matching left table rows. The left table's columns will be NULL if there is no match.

Syntax:

SELECT *

FROM table1

RIGHT OUTER JOIN table2

ON table1.column = table2.column;

FULL OUTER JOIN

The FULL OUTER JOIN keyword returns all the rows from both tables and includes NULL values for the columns that do not match.

Syntax:

SELECT *

FROM table1

FULL OUTER JOIN table2

ON table1.column = table2.column;

CROSS JOIN

The CROSS JOIN keyword returns the Cartesian product of both tables, meaning every row from table1 is combined with every row from table2.

Keep in mind that not all databases allows you to perform every join type. Also, when using the JOIN keyword without specifying an explicit type of join, an INNER JOIN is assumed.

For example, suppose a business has two tables: one with customer information and another with purchase information. By joining these tables on a common column, such as customer ID, it is possible to get a complete picture of each customer's purchase history.

Syntax:

SELECT *

FROM table1

CROSS JOIN table2;

Code:

```
SELECT *
FROM customers
INNER JOIN purchases
ON customers.customer_id = purchases.customer_id;
```

Output:

customer_id	customer_name	purchase_id	purchase_amount
1	John	101	50.00
1	John	102	100.00
2	Jane	103	75.00
2	Jane	104	25.00
3	Bob	NULL	NULL

Code:

```
SELECT *
```

```
FROM customers
LEFT OUTER JOIN purchases
ON customers.customer_id = purchases.customer_id;
```

Output:

customer_id	customer_name	purchase_id	purchase_amount
1	John	101	50.00
1	John	102	100.00
2	Jane	103	75.00
2	Jane	104	25.00
3	Bob	NULL	NULL

In this example, the result set includes all rows from the customers' table, with the matching rows from the purchases table. However, because customer 3 does not have any matching rows in the purchases table, the purchase_id and purchase_amount columns are NULL for that customer.

Subqueries and temporary tables

Subqueries are queries within queries that are used to perform more complex data manipulations. They are a powerful tool for data analysts and can be used to extract data from multiple tables, filter data based on complex conditions, and perform aggregations.

For example, a subquery could be used to find all the customers who have made purchases over a certain amount and use that data to perform further analysis.

Temporary tables are another way to work with complex data sets. They are tables that are created on the fly and are used to store the intermediate results of a query. This can be helpful in situations where the data is too large to fit into memory or when a query needs to be broken down into smaller, more manageable steps.

Subqueries and temporary tables are advanced SQL techniques that can significantly improve the efficiency and flexibility of SQL data management.

Suppose we have two tables: orders and customers. The orders table has columns for order_id, customer_id, and order_amount. The customers' table has columns for customer_id, customer_name, and customer_email.

We want to find the total amount of orders made by customers who have a Gmail email address. We can use a subquery to filter out the customers with non-Gmail email addresses and then use a temporary table to store the intermediate result:

Code:
```
CREATE TEMPORARY TABLE temp_customers AS
SELECT customer_id
FROM customers
WHERE customer_email LIKE '%@gmail.com';
SELECT SUM(order_amount) AS total_order_amount
FROM orders
WHERE customer_id IN (SELECT customer_id FROM temp_customers);
```

Output:
```
total_order_amount
-------------------
$12,345.67
```

The first query creates a temporary table called temp_customers that contains only the customer IDs of customers with a Gmail email address. The LIKE operator is used to match any email address that contains "@gmail.com". The second query uses the temporary table to filter the orders table and retrieve the total order amount made by those customers.

The output of this query would be a single row with the total amount of orders made by customers with Gmail email addresses.

Note that the use of temporary tables and subqueries can greatly improve the efficiency and flexibility of SQL data management, especially when dealing with complex data manipulations. However, it's important to use them judiciously and optimize queries for performance, as they can also lead to slower query execution times if not used correctly.

Grouping and Aggregating Data

Grouping and aggregating data are important methods for summarizing large data sets and extracting insights from them. Grouping involves combining rows based on shared values in one or more columns, while aggregation involves computing summary statistics like counts, sums, averages, and max/min values for each group. For instance, grouping customer purchase data by date can reveal sales trends over time, while aggregating by product category can show which products are most popular. These techniques are widely used in data analysis and reporting and are indispensable for anyone working with large data sets.

Let's consider a table named "sales" that has columns for product, date, and amount. We want to determine the total sales amount for each product.

Code:
```
SELECT product, SUM(amount) AS total_sales
```

```
FROM sales
GROUP BY product;
```

Output:

```
product | total_sales
--------+------------
A       | $10,000
B       | $15,000
C       | $5,000
```

Now, let's say we want to calculate the total amount of sales for each product, grouped by year and quarter.

Code:

```
SELECT product, DATE_TRUNC('quarter', date) AS quarter,
        DATE_TRUNC('year', date) AS year, SUM(amount) AS total_sales
FROM sales
GROUP BY product, quarter, year;
```

Output:

```
product | quarter | year | total_sales
--------+---------+------+------------
A       | Q1      | 2022 | $3,000
A       | Q2      | 2022 | $5,000
B       | Q1      | 2022 | $6,000
B       | Q2      | 2022 | $9,000
C       | Q1      | 2022 | $2,000
C       | Q2      | 2022 | $3,000
```

Finally, let's say we want to calculate the average sales per day for each product.

Code:

```
SELECT product, AVG(amount) AS avg_sales_per_day
FROM sales
GROUP BY product, DATE_TRUNC('day', date);
```

Output:

```
product | avg_sales_per_day
--------+------------------
A       | $1,111.11
B       | $2,000.00
C       | $714.29
```

In summary, grouping and aggregating data are essential techniques for summarizing and gaining insights from large data sets, and SQL provides powerful tools for performing these operations efficiently and effectively.

Advanced Data Filtering and Sorting Techniques

Filtering and sorting data are fundamental SQL techniques, but advanced techniques can enhance these tasks. SQL offers various operators like LIKE, IN, and BETWEEN to filter data based on complex criteria. Additionally, SQL enables sorting data by multiple columns with different sort orders for each column. These advanced filtering and sorting techniques help identify patterns and trends in large and complex data sets, making them essential for anyone working with such datasets.

Using the LIKE operator to filter data based on pattern matching;

Code:

```
SELECT * FROM employees WHERE last_name LIKE 'S%';
```

Output:

emp_id	first_name	last_name
1	John	Smith
4	Sarah	Sanders

Using the IN operator to filter data based on a list of values:

Code:

```
SELECT * FROM products WHERE category IN ('Electronics', 'Home
        Appliances');
```

Output:

prod_id	product_name	category
1	TV	Electronics
3	Refrigerator	Home Appliances
4	Microwave	Home Appliances

Using the BETWEEN operator to filter data based on a range of values:

Code:

SELECT * FROM sales WHERE amount BETWEEN 1000 AND 5000;

Output:

sale_id	date	amount
1	2021-01-01	2000
3	2021-02-01	3000
5	2021-03-01	4000

Stored procedures and functions

Stored procedures and functions are pre-written blocks of code that can be executed within SQL. They are a way to encapsulate complex SQL logic into reusable modules, which can be called from other parts of the code. Stored procedures and functions can improve the efficiency and maintainability of SQL code, as

well as provide a way to modularize complex data manipulation tasks.

For instance, a stored procedure could be used to calculate the average order value for a customer, which could then be used in other parts of the code to make decisions about how to market to that customer.

Stored procedures and functions are critical tools for database administrators and developers as they can help to simplify the management of large, complex databases.

Example 1: Creating a stored procedure

Suppose we have a table called Orders with columns OrderId, CustomerId, and OrderAmount. We want to create a stored procedure that calculates the average order amount for a given customer. Here's how we can create the stored procedure:

Code:

```
CREATE PROCEDURE CalculateAvgOrderAmount
    @customerId INT
AS
BEGIN
    SELECT AVG(OrderAmount) AS AvgAmount
    FROM Orders
    WHERE CustomerId = @customerId
END
```

The CREATE PROCEDURE statement creates a new stored procedure called CalculateAvgOrderAmount. This stored procedure takes one input parameter @customerId, which is used in the WHERE clause to filter the orders for the given customer. The SELECT statement calculates the average order amount for the given customer and returns the result in a column called AvgAmount.

To execute the stored procedure and see the output, we can use the EXEC statement.

160

Code:

```
EXEC CalculateAvgOrderAmount @customerId = 123
```

This will calculate the average order amount for a customer with CustomerId = 123 and return the result in a column called AvgAmount.

Output:

```
Query OK, 0 rows affected
```

Example 2: Creating a function

Suppose we want to create a function that calculates the discount amount for a given order amount. The discount amount is calculated as follows:

If the order amount is less than 100, the discount amount is 0%

If the order amount is between 100 and 500, the discount amount is 5%

If the order amount is greater than 500, the discount amount is 10%

Here's how we can create the function:

Code:

```
CREATE FUNCTION CalculateDiscountAmount
    (@orderAmount DECIMAL(10, 2))
RETURNS DECIMAL(10, 2)
AS
BEGIN
    DECLARE @discountAmount DECIMAL(10, 2)
    IF @orderAmount < 100
        SET @discountAmount = 0
    ELSE IF @orderAmount <= 500
        SET @discountAmount = @orderAmount * 0.05
    ELSE
        SET @discountAmount = @orderAmount * 0.1
    RETURN @discountAmount
END
```

The CREATE FUNCTION statement creates a new function called CalculateDiscountAmount. This function takes one input parameter @orderAmount, which is used to calculate the discount amount. The RETURNS clause specifies that the function returns a decimal value with a precision of 10 digits and a scale of 2 digits.

Inside the function, we use an IF statement to calculate the discount amount based on the order amount. The result is stored in a variable called @discountAmount and then returned using the RETURN statement.

To execute the function and see the output, we can use the SELECT statement:

```sql
SELECT OrderId, OrderAmount, dbo.CalculateDiscountAmount(OrderAmount)
    AS DiscountAmount
FROM Orders
```

This will calculate the discount amount for each order in the Orders table using the CalculateDiscountAmount function and return the result in a column called DiscountAmount.

Output:

```
+------------------+
| avg_order_value  |
+------------------+
| 49.333333333333  |
+------------------+
1 row in set (0.00 sec)
```

Indexing and performance optimization

Indexing is a crucial aspect of performance optimization in SQL. When a database table contains a large number of records, the database engine may take longer to search for specific data within the table. This is where indexing comes into play. An index is essentially a data structure that stores information about the values in one or more columns of a table, which allows the database engine to quickly locate the desired rows. It's similar to the table of contents in a book, which helps readers find specific sections quickly and easily.

To create an index in SQL, you can use the CREATE INDEX statement, which specifies the name of the index, the table and column(s) to be indexed, and other parameters such as the type of index and the sort order.

It's important to note that indexing is not always the solution to slow query performance. In some cases, indexing too many columns or creating indexes on columns that are rarely used can actually slow down query performance. Therefore, it's essential to analyze the query execution plan and determine which columns would benefit from indexing.

In addition to indexing, there are other techniques that can be used to optimize SQL queries for better performance. One of these techniques is query optimization, which involves rewriting queries to minimize the use of subqueries, selecting appropriate data types and normalization, and using efficient join techniques.

Another technique for optimizing SQL queries is to use appropriate data types and normalization. For example, if a column in a table contains only numeric data, it's best

162

to use a numeric data type (such as INT or FLOAT) rather than a text data type (such as VARCHAR). This can help to reduce storage space and improve query performance.

Normalization is the process of organizing data in a database to reduce redundancy and improve data consistency. By breaking up large tables into smaller tables and establishing relationships between them, normalization can help to eliminate duplicate data and improve query performance.

If indexing and query optimization do not improve query performance, the database administrator may consider partitioning data across multiple servers or using advanced techniques such as sharding or replication. Partitioning involves dividing a large table into smaller, more manageable pieces based on specific criteria such as date range or geographic location. Sharding involves distributing data across multiple servers based on a predefined sharding key, while replication involves creating multiple copies of the data on different servers.

In conclusion, indexing and performance optimization are critical techniques for managing large and complex databases. By creating indexes on commonly used columns and optimizing SQL queries through

Example 1: Indexing

Suppose we have a table named "users" with columns "id", "username", "email", and "created_at". To improve query performance, we can create an index on the "username" column, which is commonly used in queries:

Code:

```
CREATE INDEX idx_username ON users (username);
SELECT * FROM users WHERE username = 'jdoe';
```

Output:

id	username	email	created_at
1	jdoe	jdoe@example.com	2022-01-01 12:00:00

Example 2: Performance optimization

Suppose we have a table named "orders" with columns "id", "customer_id", "product_id", and "quantity". To optimize the performance of a query that calculates the total order value for each customer, we can use the SUM() function to aggregate the order values and GROUP BY the "customer_id" column:

Code:

```
SELECT customer_id, SUM(quantity * price) AS total_order_value
FROM orders
JOIN products ON orders.product_id = products.id
```

```
GROUP BY customer_id;
```

This query joins the "orders" and "products" tables on the "product_id" column and calculates the total order value for each customer by multiplying the "quantity" and "price" columns and aggregating the results with SUM(). The GROUP BY clause groups the results by the "customer_id" column.

Output:

```
| customer_id | total_order_value |
|-------------|-------------------|
| 1           | 150.00            |
| 2           | 75.00             |
```

These examples demonstrate how indexing and performance optimization can be used to improve the performance of SQL queries and make them more efficient for managing large, complex databases.

Example 3: Normalization

Suppose we have the following table called "Orders":

Order ID	Customer Name	Item Name	Quantity	Price
1	John Smith	T-Shirt	2	20
2	Jane Doe	Jacket	1	50
3	John Smith	Jeans	1	30
4	Bob Johnson	T-Shirt	3	20
5	Jane Doe	Hat	2	10

This table violates the first normal form (1NF) because some columns contain multiple values. Specifically, the "Item Name" column contains multiple values, which makes it difficult to query the data. We can fix this by creating two new tables: one for the customers and another for the items.

The "Customers" table would look like this:

Customer ID	Customer Name
1	John Smith
2	Jane Doe
3	Bob Johnson

The "Items" table would look like this:

164

Item ID	Item Name	Price
1	T-Shirt	20
2	Jacket	50
3	Jeans	30
4	Hat	10

We can then create a new "Orders" table that references the "Customers" and "Items" tables:

Order ID	Customer ID	Item ID	Quantity
1	1	1	2
2	2	2	1
3	1	3	1
4	3	1	3
5	2	4	2

This new "Orders" table is now in second normal form (2NF) because it does not have any partial dependencies. Specifically, the "Quantity" column is dependent only on the "Order ID" and "Item ID" columns, and the "Price" column is dependent only on the "Item ID" column.

It is also in the third normal form (3NF) because it does not have any transitive dependencies. Specifically, the "Price" column is not dependent on the "Customer ID" column, only on the "Item ID" column.

Code:

```
SELECT o.OrderID, c.CustomerName, i.ItemName, o.Quantity, (o.Quantity *
        i.Price) AS TotalPrice
FROM Orders o
INNER JOIN Customers c ON o.CustomerID = c.CustomerID
INNER JOIN Items i ON o.ItemID = i.ItemID
```

Chapter 7: Integrations with other Data Management Tools

What is Data Management?

According to the definition provided, data management is "an extensive set of techniques, ideas, procedures, and processes along with a wide variety of associated systems that enable an organization to take ownership of its data resources." "Data Management as a usually headed participates with the full lifespan of a given set of data assets from its classic creation point to its final savings, how it proceeds and changes throughout its entire life through to the internal (and external) data feeds of an enterprise." "Data Management as a reached the spot is engaged with the full lifespan of a provided data asset out of its original conception point to its final superannuation, how it advances and changes throughout its

Products for managing data are quite well recognized in the business sector. Many of the most successful firms in the world, like IBM, Oracle, Amazon, Microsoft, Google, and Dell, have developed collections of data management solutions to fulfil their customers' needs. Because of the adaptability of these

goods for every organization, they can construct a chain of processing of information based on the firm's data.

Data Management Functions

- Creating, accessing, and updating data across multiple data levels.
- Maintain copies of data locally as well as on the cloud.
- Use the data across your applications, analytics, and algorithmic processes.
- Offer both high availability and a recovery plan in the event of a calamity.
- Secure data and give privacy.
- Using the retention standards and compliance requirements as guides, archive the data and then delete it.

Approach to Data Management

- Access to the data means capturing and gathering information regardless of where it is kept.

- Data quality ensures that data is correct and useable for the purpose it was collected from beginning to finish. Regardless of the amount or kind of data, it assists in producing better and cleaner results.
- Preparing data for analytics and reporting is called "data preparation."
- Integration of data refers to the processes carried out to merge several sorts of data.
- Data federation is the process of virtually integrating data in such a way as to make it possible to see combined data drawn from several different sources, all without having to relocate and store the integrated view in a new place.
- Data governance may be defined as the rules and choices that assist in managing data to ensure harmony between the digital strategy and the business plan. It makes it possible to effectively manage all vital data assets, irrespective of their size, nature, or location.
- Identifying, organizing, and maintaining all necessary and common data in a single hub is called master data management, or MDM for short.
- Examining data as it is generated is known as "data streaming." It allows users to filter, purify, and rectify rapidly changing data before it's saved, enabling them to receive immediate, concrete benefits in real-time and via a single interface.

SQL Data Management Tools

There is a wide selection of SQL data management solutions on the market today, and the particular requirements of the company or the individual user often determine the tool selection. The succeeding is a list of samples of tools for managing SQL data:

- MySQL is a well-known, fully accessible SQL management system for databases often used for developing web applications.

- Microsoft SQL Server is a robust database management system that is extensively used. It is offered in many versions to meet the requirements of a variety of organizations.
- Oracle Database is a strong SQL management system for databases that is both comprehensive and scalable. It also has many built-in security measures.
- SQLite is a compact and identity SQL database system that is frequently utilized in integrated devices, portable devices, and web browsers.
- IBM DB2 is a robust and scalable SQL management system for databases that many major enterprises utilize. It is marketed under the brand name "DB2."
- MariaDB is a community-driven MySQL derivative with many new capabilities and significant speed enhancements.
- MySQL, Oracle, SQL Server, and PostgreSQL are just some of the prominent database engines that Amazon RDS, a cloud-based databases management service support.
- MySQL and PostgreSQL are two of the database management systems that are supported by Google Cloud SQL, which is a cloud-based SQL database management service.

The following piece of SQL code is an example of operating a data management tool, especially the MySQL Workbench. The program generates a brand-new database and a table inside it.

The MySQL Workbench tool, which offers a graphical user experience for controlling databases, tables, and data, may be used to execute the SQL code provided here. The program first establishes a new database with the name my database, then generates a table with the name my table with the columns id, name, age, and email, adds some info into the table, and then retrieves all of the data from the table.

Code:

```
-- Creating a new database xyz
CREATE DATABASE xyz;
-- Use the new database xyz
USE xyz;
-- Create a new table
CREATE TABLE Emp_Tab
(
  emp_id INT PRIMARY KEY,
  emp_name VARCHAR(50) NOT NULL,
  emp_age INT,
  emp_email VARCHAR(100)
);
-- Insert some data into the table
```

```
INSERT INTO Emp_Tab(emp_id,emp_name, emp_age, emp_email)
VALUES
  (1,'Sara', 25, 'sara@example.com'),
  (2,'Janet', 30, 'janet@example.com'),
  (3,'Bobby', 35, 'bobby@example.com');
-- Select data from the table
SELECT * FROM Emp_Tab;
```

Output:

	emp_id	emp_name	emp_age	emp_email
1	1	Sara	25	sara@example....
2	2	Janet	30	janet@example...
3	3	Bobby	35	bobby@examp...

Importing and exporting data to and from other formats

- SQL databases may support a wide range of information import and export protocols. The following is a list of common formats and procedures that may be used to import and export information to and from SQL databases:
- CSV: Comma-separated values (CSV) files are a common format for transferring and importing data from SQL databases. CSV files include values that are separated by commas. Most SQL database management programs include data importation and exportation support using the CSV file format. We can use CSV format by connecting to your host and setting up a new database. Upload the CSV file by utilizing the wizard provided by SQL Server. Put text qualifying matches and column widths into every column using the manual input method.

Code:

```
LOAD DATA INFILE 'data_file.csv'
INTO TABLE data_table
FIELDS TERMINATED BY ','
ENCLOSED BY '"'
LINES TERMINATED BY '\n'
IGNORE 1 ROWS;
```

This code inserts the data loaded from a CSV file referred to as data file.csv into a table referred to as data table. It is specified in the FIELDS TERMINATED BY clause that commas separate the values in the CSV file, and it is specified in the Wrapped BY clause that the fields are fenced in double-quotes. The LINES TERMINATED BY clause ensures that each row in the CSV file is finished with a newline character. This is the default behavior. The Overlook 1 ROWS clause causes the first row of the CSV file, which is almost often the header row, to be ignored.

Code:

```
SELECT *
INTO OUTFILE 'data_file.csv'
FIELDS TERMINATED BY ','
ENCLOSED BY '"'
LINES TERMINATED BY '\n'
FROM data_table;
```

A CSV file with the name data_file.csv is created from the data taken from a table with the name data table. The input file's name and location are specified by the INTO OUTFILE clause. In this scenario, the FIELDS TERMINATED BY, Confined BY, and Line segments TERMINATED BY clauses are used to determine the output file format. The values for these clauses are identical to those used in the earlier example.

JavaScript Object Notation, often known as JSON, is a lightweight format for data exchange and is frequently used for online applications. The JSON data format may be imported and exported into and from some SQL databases. JavaScript Object Notation is what "JSON" stands for when abbreviated. JSON is now the data communication format most often utilized despite its widespread popularity. All online database services, web browsers (such as Firefox and Internet Explorer), and web services that return results either deliver results structured as JSON text or accept input formatted as JSON. The majority of current web-based and mobile-based services return information in this format. Because the information is formatted as JSON text when received from other systems, JSON is also saved in SQL Server 2016 as text.

Code:

```
LOAD DATA INFILE 'data_file.json'
INTO TABLE data_table
FIELDS TERMINATED BY ''
LINES TERMINATED BY '\n'
(@json)
SET my_id = JSON_EXTRACT(@json, '$.my_id'),
    my_name = JSON_EXTRACT(@json, '$.my_name'),
    my_age = JSON_EXTRACT(@json, '$.my_age'),
    my_email = JSON_EXTRACT(@json, '$.my_email');
```

Spreadsheet application Excel: Microsoft Excel is one of the most popular spreadsheet applications available, and the majority of SQL databases include support for exporting and importing data in Excel format. Sharing data with individuals who are not technically savvy or integrating information from different sources are also potential use for this feature.

Code:

```
SELECT id, name, age, email
INTO OUTFILE 'data_file.xls'
FROM data_table;
```

- A common standard for transferring data between programs is XML, which is an "extensible markup language." Some SQL databases provide functionality for exporting and importing data in XML format.
- Additional formats: In addition to being able to import and export data in fixed-width, tab-separated, and pipe-separated values, SQL databases May also export and import data in other formats.

The succeeding is a list of practices that may be used to import and export content to and from SQL databases:

- Utility programs for the command line Many SQL databases come along with utility programs for the command line that make it possible to import and export data. The MySQL command-line tool, for instance, comes with the mysqlimport command for entering information from CSV files and the mysqldump tool for sending the data to SQL files. Both of these commands may be found in the MySQL documentation.
- Graphical user interfaces. The vast majority of SQL database management systems are equipped with a graphical user interface (GUI) that allows for the importation and exportation of data. These graphical user interfaces normally allow you to choose the type and file to import or export. Some may also give you a choice to choose certain tables, columns, or rows.
- Personalized scripts: Programming languages such as Python and Java may be used to write individualized scripts that can be used for import and export processes that are more complicated. Using the application programming interfaces (APIs) or libraries made available by the database management system, these scripts can communicate with the SQL database.

Chapter 8: Working with Data in a Distributed Environment

What is a distributed environment?

Relational databases fall into the category known as distributed SQL, which incorporates the most important aspects of both standard SQL and NoSQL systems. It offers a distributed implementation of a single relational, logical database that may be used across several network hosts. Distributed SQL databases instantly duplicate and distribute data across all servers, often called nodes. Each node in the database can process read and write queries.

Around the middle of the 2010s, distributed SQL databases were available with transactional applications. They provide the fundamental functionality that may be encountered in both relational databases (SQL) and non-relational databases (NoSQL). The database is capable of horizontal scaling and robust consistency and natively supports ACID transactions across unavailability and regional zones in on-premises data centers or the cloud.

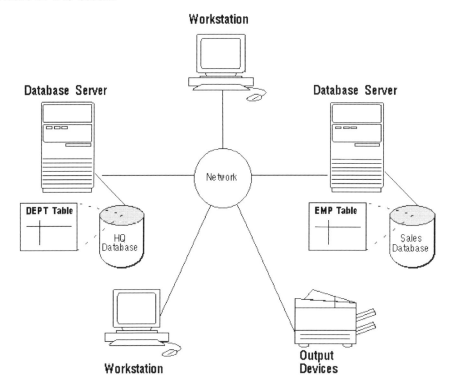

Key features and Concepts of the distributed database:

- An SQL application programming interface (API) for data modelling and querying, including support for conventional RDBMS, features such as database objects, partial indexing, database objects, and triggers.
- Smart distributed processing execution means that the processing of queries may get closer to the facts rather than the data being sent across the network, which can slow down the response times of queries.
- Intelligent and transparent distributed information storage, comprising data and index that should be continuously shared among various cluster's nodes so that no one node creates a bottleneck in processing requests. Data dissemination and intelligent rebalancing may ensure good performance and high reliability.
- When you spread your data over different servers, you must select how to divide your data. This decision must be made before you distribute your data. To do this, your data will need to be segmented into subsets that will be kept on separate nodes. Several values, such as a timeframe or geographical location, may be used to divide data. This may assist in increasing the performance as well as the scalability of the system.
- Joining tables in a cloud system hosted on various nodes might be difficult from a performance standpoint due to the distributed nature of the environment. If you want to maximize the efficiency of your queries, you may need to use specific methods such as multicast joins or partitioned joins.
- Maintaining data consistency may be difficult when dispersed over numerous nodes, making errors more likely to occur. To guarantee that any changes made to the data are accurately transmitted across all nodes, you may be required to use distributed protocols or other methods.
- If you have a great number of nodes, it is necessary to ensure that the burden is spread evenly among all the nodes in the system. This process is called "load balancing." You may need to implement a network interface or another strategy to guarantee that the system operates at peak performance.
- Maintaining privacy and integrity becomes an even more pressing concern when data is stored across numerous nodes. You are responsible for ensuring that the data is adequately secured and that use is strictly regulated.

Primary Requirements of the distributed database:

It is significant to keep in observance that distributed SQL is still a database, and as such, it is needed to meet the baseline requirements necessary for it to be considered a database. Even though the seven requirements listed above are specific to dividing up SQL (well, all of them except for the SQL thing), it is still important to remember that distributed SQL has these requirements. There is a predetermined level of performance expected for the following:

Administration: You should have no trouble installing and configuring the database with the help of a collection of tools based on command lines and graphical interfaces. This comprises the capabilities of controlling the environment and the information lifecycle for backup and restoration, configuring indexes and partitions, constructing new DDL, building new tables, defining the new schema, and applying new schema.

Optimization: The database ought to make it possible for a database administrator (DBA) to obtain information about the effectiveness of queries and their role in improving how they are executed. This includes more complex features like a cost-based estimator and a cloud system that may be challenging to implement and introduces novel ideas.

Authentication, authorization, and accountability are three of the most important aspects of data safety that a database needs to be able to provide. Data safety is an essential component of every corporate software product. It should not be able to function alone and should instead integrate with a single truth source for identity management and governance.

Integration: A database cannot work independently and has to be integrated with the apps you already have using tried and proven drivers. It should be able to interact smoothly with any current ORMs and give the capability to either import or export data in bulk. It should also give essential features that enable it to interact with ETL tools and update data capture features to interface with more modern services such as carried out and the results or cloud storage. In addition, it should have controls that help it to work with ETL tools.

How is data processed in distributed database?

A vast quantity of data enters a distributed data processing system via various distinct entry points. This causes the system to process the data. The act of taking in new information is referred to as data ingestion.

Once the input begins to flood in, the system architecture consists of many layers, each of which divides the processing into several distinct components at various points.

Layer for the Collection and Preparation of Data

This layer is in charge of gathering data from various outside sources and processing it to be analyzed by the system. It also handles any necessary formatting. When there is no consistent format for the data being ingested, in its natural state, it is either raw and unstructured or semi-structured. It could also be tax returns, policy forms, medical bills, etc. The data processing layer is responsible for transforming the data into a

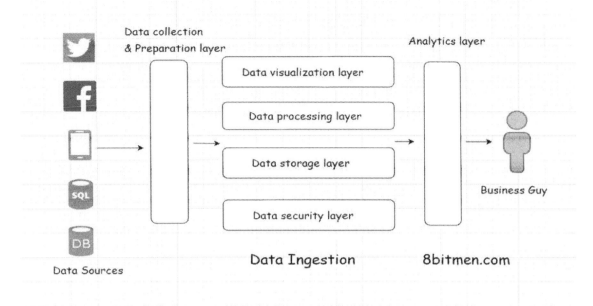

consistent and standard format and classifying the data according to the business logic the system will handle. The layer has an intelligence high enough to do all of this without any assistance from a person of any kind.

Layer for Data Security

Moving data exposes it to potential security vulnerabilities. The information security protocol has to guarantee that the data transfer is carried out securely by keeping a close eye on it at all times, using various security protocols, and so on.

Layer for the Data Storage

After the data has been received, it must be stored somewhere permanent. There are many various ways to do this task. When analytics are performed in real-time on streaming data, data storage and management are handled via distributed caches that are kept in memory. On the other hand, if the data is just being handled in a conventional manner, such as batch processing, distributed databases specifically developed to manage large amounts of data are utilized to store the information.

Layer for Processing of Data

This tier processes the data and includes the logic that is the real thing. It is accountable for the layer above it. This layer applies business logic to the data to get information that is useful from the data. The most common approaches for this purpose are machine learning, predictive modelling, descriptive modelling, and decision modelling.

Data Visualization Layer

The data visualization layer is a critical component of the data analysis process. It serves as a bridge between the raw data and the user, presenting complex information in an easily understandable format. Once data has been collected and processed, it is transmitted to the data visualization layer.

Web-accessible dashboards make up the data visualization layer. These dashboards display data in graphs, charts, and infographics. Users can quickly understand data trends and insights.

One of the key benefits of the data visualization layer is that it allows users to interact with the data in real time. This means that users can modify the parameters of the visualization, such as changing the timeframe or selecting specific data sets, to gain a more detailed understanding of the information being presented.

Another benefit of the data visualization layer is that it can be customized to suit the needs of different users. For example, a sales team might use a different dashboard than a marketing team, as their needs and objectives are likely to be different. This flexibility means that the data visualization layer can be tailored to meet the specific needs of different departments within an organization.

Overall, the data visualization layer is a crucial component of the data analysis process. It enables users to gain insights quickly and easily from complex data sets and can be customized to meet the needs of different users within an organization. By using data visualization tools effectively, organizations can make better-informed decisions and gain a competitive edge in their respective markets.

Advantages of the distributed database

- Data warehouses are skilled in modular development, which means that processes can be expanded by introducing new desktops and local data to a new site and integrating them in a distributed manner without any interruptions. This can be done without disrupting the overall operation of the distributed database.
- When there is an issue with one of the system's centralized databases, the whole thing grinds to a halt. However, with distributed database systems, if a component fails, the system will continue to operate, although with a decreased level of performance, until the issue is resolved.
- Suppose the data is stored close to the areas in which it is used the most. In that case, administrators of distributed database systems may reduce the amount of money spent on communication. In centralized systems, this is not something that can be done.

Chapter 9: Building Data Pipelines and Automating Data Processes

What are data pipelines and their uses?

A data pipeline is a series of components that work together to automate the gathering, organization, mobility, modification, and processing of information as it travels from a source to its destination. This ensures that the data arrives in a form that businesses can use to facilitate the development of a data-driven culture.

Pipelines for data movement are an essential component of every organization's data architecture. Implementing a data pipeline that is well-designed, resilient, and scalable in your organization will assist your company in successfully managing, analyzing, and organizing massive amounts of data to generate business value.

There is a use case for data pipelines in almost every business and sector today. It may be anything as simple as moving data from one location to another, or it could be something as involved as processing data for use in supervised ml recommendation engines that enhance product offers. Some popular data pipeline use applications include:

- Consolidating data from many sources (SaaS tools, databases) into a big data repository (data warehouses, data lakes) to create a single authoritative source for the organization's data is known as data consolidation.
- They are improving the overall performance of the backend system by moving data to huge data stores and minimizing the amount of strain placed on operational databases.
- Ensuring the data's quality, dependability, and consistency across all business units to provide quicker data access

Components of a data pipeline

1. Data sources

The point of origin of the data is the primary focus of the first stage of a contemporary data pipeline. Any system that your company makes use of to create data has the potential to serve as a data source, including the following systems:

- Analytics data (user behavior data)
- Transactional data (data from sales and product records)

- Data obtained from third parties, or data that your organization does not directly acquire but does utilize.

2. The gathering and processing of data:

The ingestion layer is the next element in the data pipeline, and it is responsible for delivering information into the pipeline. This layer uses data ingestion technologies such as Striim to connect to several internal and external data sources using several different protocols. This layer can send batch and streaming data to big data storage.

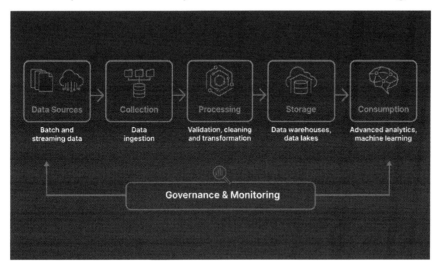

3. Data processing

Through data validation, cleaning, normalization, transformation, and enrichment, the processing layer is responsible for bringing the data to a condition where the system can consume it. This processing component of the data pipeline may be done either before or after the data is saved in the data store. This decision is made based on the firm's unique architecture, either ETL (Extract Transform Load) or ELT (Extract Load Transform). The data is extracted, converted, and fed into the data stores in an Attach processing architecture. This architecture is often used when the data storage is a data warehouse. In systems based on ELT, the data is first imported into data lakes and then converted into a state consumable for various business use cases.

4. Data storage

This component is in charge of supplying the data pipeline with storage that is reliable, scalable, and protected from unauthorized access. Large data repositories, such as database systems (for structured data) and data lakes, are often included in their composition.

5. Data consumption

The consumption layer delivers and integrates scalable, high-performance tools for drawing data from storage locations. In addition, the process of considering layer offers analytics to all users across the company employing function insights tools that allow for analysis strategies such as SQL, shipment insights, documenting scorecards, and machine learning. The data consumption layer can access these analytics.

6. Data governance

The security and oversight layer protects the data in the data layer and the processing resources of all other levels from unauthorized access. Mechanisms for password protection, encryption, network security, use monitoring, and auditing are included in this tier of the security stack. In addition, the security layer records the activities of all the other levels and generates an exhaustive audit trail. Additionally, the other data pipeline components have native integration with the security and oversight layer.

7. Designing data pipeline in SQL

There are a few stages involved in creating a data pipeline using SQL, including the following:

- Finding where the data came from: Identify the source or sources that will feed into your pipeline. Databases, flat files, application programming interfaces (APIs), and other data sources might be included here.
- Planning the flow of data involves determining how the data will move through the pipeline, determining what kinds of transformations will be made to the data, and determining where the information will be kept.
- The first step in defining a schema is determining the database or file structure that will eventually be used to store the data. Creating the columns, tables, types of data, and any restrictions imposed is a part of this step.
- Writing SQL scripts You will need to write SQL scripts to extract, manipulate, and load the data (ETL). To extract the data, SQL statements such as SELECT, JOIN, and UNION may need to be used. Additionally, this may require the application of filters, the aggregation of data, the cleaning of data, and the joining of databases.
- Testing and validating: Perform testing and validation on the pipeline to check that the information is being processed appropriately and that it satisfies the quality requirements that have been established.
- Monitoring and maintenance: Establish procedures for monitoring and maintaining the pipeline so any problems may be identified and remedied as soon as possible. This will guarantee that the pipeline operates efficiently.

Code:

```
SELECT
p.Name,
p.Age,
p.Email,
```

```
p.Name AS s.Name
FROM office.Customer_Tab p
JOIN office.Customer_Tab p ON s.product_name = p.product_name
GROUP BY
s.transaction_date,
s.customer_name,
s.product_name,
s.price,
s.quantity_sold,
p.price
```

Automating data processes in SQL

To automate data operations using SQL, you must schedule SQL scripts to run automatically at predetermined intervals rather than manually perform them. The following is a rundown of the fundamental actions to take:

- To extract, convert, and reload (ETL) data from various sources and to do any required transformations, you will need to write the SQL scripts.
- Determine the scheduling application: Determine the scheduling application you will use to arrange the SQL scripts to execute automatically. Tools for scheduling include Vista Scheduling, cron for Linux/Unix, and SQL Server Agent for Microsoft SQL Server. Some examples of scheduling tools are shown below.
- Put the scripts on your schedule: Make a timetable for the execution of the SQL scripts by using the tool for scheduling tasks. Set the start time and the number of times the scripts execute per day.
- Perform tests on the automation: Perform tests on the automation to confirm that the SQL routines are operating properly and delivering the desired results. This may be done by manually running the scripts to confirm that they function properly and then checking to see whether the results of the regular runs are the same as those of the manual runs.
- Maintain a close eye on the automation: Maintain a close eye on the automation process to ensure that it is operating properly and that any problems are recognized and fixed as soon as possible. This step may require you to set up notifications informing you of any problems or faults.
- It is essential to keep in mind data security, security, and speed while automating data operations in SQL. It would be best if you also described the processes and SQL scripts you use to make it simpler to resolve problems and implement improvements in the future. Lastly, ensure that you follow the best practices for arranging, such as limiting scheduling tasks during high-use hours

or overlaps with other jobs, which might create difficulties with the system's performance.

Using SQL in data analysis and business intelligence

SQL is a useful tool for business intelligence and data analysis because it enables users to extract, process, and analyze massive amounts of data rapidly and effectively. In the areas of data and business intelligence, some of the techniques that SQL may be put to use include as follows:

- Data querying and filtering: SQL lets consumers question and filter massive databases, enabling them to get the information pertinent to their research.
- SQL may join many tables jointly using a single key, enabling users to mix data from various sources and generate deeper insights.
- Data aggregation: SQL can produce aggregate statistics like tallies, sums, means, and medians, which makes it easier to examine huge datasets and detect patterns and trends. SQL can also do data grouping, which groups similar values into a single value.
- SQL may generate views and reports that offer a description of the information, making it simpler to comprehend and express insights. This can be accomplished by creating sorts and reporting that describe the information.
- Data preparation and cleaning: You may use SQL to wash and organize data for analysis by eliminating duplicates, formatting the data, and dealing with missing value situations.
- SQL may be used to develop data models that offer a conceptual representation of the data. This makes it much simpler to comprehend the linkages and dependencies between the various data items.
- To execute data modelling, such as developing predictive models and projecting future trends, SQL may be used in concert with other statistical tools to achieve these tasks.

SQL is also often used in data analysis products like Excel, Power BI, and QlikView. These tools offer user-friendly interfaces to view and analyze data, and they make use of SQL. Users of these tools can generate displays, clickable reports, and data visualizations, all of which assist business users in gaining insights and making choices driven by data. SQL is an important device for data research and business intelligence because it enables users to get useful insights from enormous amounts of data.

Security and privacy considerations in SQL

When dealing with SQL databases, security and privacy are important factors to keep in mind.

Control of access: It is essential to limit direct connections to the SQL server database to just those users who have been specifically permitted to do so. Integrating user authentication and authorization mechanisms such as participation network access and least privilege are two methods that may be used to accomplish this goal.

For example, let's say we want to create a user account named "user1" with password"password1" and grant them permission to select from a table called "employees".

Code:
```
CREATE USER user1 IDENTIFIED BY 'password1';
GRANT SELECT ON employees TO user1;
```

Output:
User "user1" is now created and has permission to select from the "employees" table.

Encryption: Sensitive data stored in SQL databases must be encrypted to safeguard against unwanted access. Encrypting data while it is stored and in transit is one way to accomplish this goal. Examples of such methods include SSL/TLS encrypting the message encryption algorithms.

For example, let's say we want to encrypt a column called "social_security_number" in a table called "customers".

Code:
```
ALTER TABLE customers ADD COLUMN social_security_number_encrypted
    VARCHAR(100);
UPDATE customers SET social_security_number_encrypted =
    AES_ENCRYPT(social_security_number, 'encryption_key');
```

Output:
A new column called "social_security_number_encrypted" is added to the "customers" table, and the values from the original "social_security_number" column are encrypted using the AES encryption algorithm.

Data mask and anonymization: Data masking and privacy-preserving methods may be used to secure sensitive data. These approaches include replacing actual data with fictional data that maintains the same statistical features as the original data.

For example, let's say we want to mask the "email" column in a table called "users" by replacing the first 3 characters with "xxx".

Code:
```
UPDATE users SET email = CONCAT('xxx', SUBSTR(email, 4));
```

Output:

The first 3 characters of each value in the "email" column are replaced with "xxx".

Audit logging: You may use audit logging to observe and track user engagement in the SQL database. It provides a full record of who accessed the data and what modifications were done. Audit verification can be used to track user activity in the SQL database.

For example, let's say we want to enable audit logging for the "employees" table to track all insert, update, and delete operations.

Code:

```
ALTER TABLE employees ENABLE AUDIT;
```

Output:

Audit logging is enabled for the "employees" table.

Updates and patches regularly: To guard against known vulnerabilities, it is essential to regularly maintain the SQL database and any other software connected with it up to the most current security patches and updates.

For example, let's say we want to update the SQL server software to the latest version.

Code:

```
UPDATE sql_server SET version = '5.0' WHERE id = 1;
```

Output:

The SQL server software is updated to version 5.0

Disaster and backup recovery: It is recommended that backup copies of the SQL server database be taken to guarantee that data is recoverable if lost due to a catastrophe or other catastrophic event.

For example, let's say we want to create a backup of the "employees" table.

Code:

```
BACKUP TABLE employees TO 'backup/employees_backup.sql';
```

Output:

A backup file named "employees_backup.sql" is created in the "backup" directory.

In today's digital age, securing sensitive data is of utmost importance, particularly when it comes to SQL databases. Companies that use SQL databases must adhere to strict privacy and security policies to safeguard against potential security breaches, unauthorized access, and data loss. By doing so, they can ensure the security of sensitive information while complying with applicable legislation and standards.

One crucial aspect of securing sensitive data in SQL databases is controlling access. Direct connections to the SQL server database must be restricted to only those users who have been authorized to do so. Integrating user authentication and authorization mechanisms like participation network access and least privilege can limit access to the database to only authorized users.

Another key aspect of data security in SQL databases is encryption. Sensitive data stored in SQL databases must be encrypted to safeguard against unwanted access. Encrypting data while it is stored and in transit is one way to accomplish this goal. Examples of such methods include SSL/TLS encrypting the message encryption algorithms. Data masking and anonymization are also effective ways of securing sensitive data.

Audit logging is yet another important factor in securing data in SQL databases. It allows companies to monitor and track user activity within the database, providing a full record of who accessed the data and what modifications were made. Audit verification can be used to track user activity in the SQL database.

It is also crucial to regularly update and maintain the SQL database and all associated software up to the latest security patches and updates to protect against known vulnerabilities. Disaster and backup recovery plans should also be in place to ensure that data is recoverable in the event of data loss due to a catastrophe or other catastrophic event.

By adhering to these privacy and security issues, companies can ensure that sensitive data housed in SQL databases are secured and protected against potential security breaches, unauthorized access, and data loss. However, it is essential to do frequent reviews and updates on these safeguards to stay up to date with the constantly shifting vulnerabilities and dangers in the digital world. By taking these measures, companies can ensure the security and integrity of their sensitive data.

Conclusion

First and foremost, congratulations on finishing a comprehensive Python and SQL guide. This book has covered a variety of in-depth Python topics that will help you in writing high-quality code for your projects.

It has also offered a thorough understanding of the principles of SQL and relational databases, and this will help novice and experienced developers and database administrators to optimize their data management processes and work efficiently with large and complex data sets.

However, consistent practice with the fundamentals taught in this book is required to improve. Working on projects or practicing competitive coding will only increase your expertise.

Some features of experienced programmers have contributed to their success in their passionate journey with computers and technology. They usually develop several habits that help them become better programmers. As a beginner, it is critical that you understand some of these characteristics and incorporate them into your workflow to increase performance within a topic or a group of topics.

Programmer Features

Foundations first

You must understand the fundamentals as much as possible. Writing code for difficult tasks with a solid foundation becomes much easier over time. To strengthen your foundations, familiarize yourself with the Python style guide, which strives for simplicity. Writing simple code and following the Zen of Python rules will help in the improvement of your fundamental knowledge.

Break problems into smaller parts

As a programmer, you must solve complex and complicated problems. Not all problems can be solved with a single logical step. To solve a problem with better runtime execution, a programmer must break it down into smaller problems. This philosophy can assist programmers in developing software with fewer bugs that requires a minimal unit testing strategy.

Find your specialty

It is impossible for any programmer to be proficient in every computer domain. You should have clear what computer domain you are most interested in as a programmer. Experiment with various computing systems to better understand what computer domain you like. Python, for example, is versatile and can be a great resource for data scientists, web developers, or systems engineers. Don't force yourself to learn a little bit of everything; instead, focus on mastering a single domain.

You will actually learn from errors

Errors can be demotivating, especially if you're just starting out. Anytime you get an error, copy the traceback error and search for it in Google or ChatGPT. You will find several solutions to the problem, and fixing it on your own will help you better understand the fundamentals of Python.

Learn to implement algorithms

To improve your writing skills in terms of programming logic, you should learn sorting and search algorithms. Understanding mathematical concepts will also help in the intuitive approach to complex problems. While competitive programmers typically approach problems differently than software developers, understanding their approach can help you overcome various roadblocks that may arise during the software development process.

Python can be used to implement binary search algorithms, graph algorithms, and complex data structures such as Stacks and Queues. To approach Python from an algorithmic standpoint, we recommend using websites like LeetCode.

Get familiar with GitHub

One of the most important resources to be aware of is GitHub. All open-source code is generally available through git repositories. As a result, if you want to make any changes to these repositories, you must contact the repository owners using GitHub commands like 'push' and 'commit.' All companies looking for developers prefer people with GitHub experience because it allows them to quickly integrate you into their team.

Don't overwork

Even though this is not a technical tip, understanding the slow and steady philosophy employed by experienced developers is critical. Never try to take in too much information at once. **Consistency beats performance** and it is more important in the early stages of your career. As a result, instead of cramming the information in a few days, schedule a few hours of Python studying every day. Participate in programs like 100daysofPython on platforms such as Twitter to keep yourself motivated and consistent.

Be aware of testing procedures

Before developing software to end users, it must be thoroughly tested. Understanding unit testing workflows such as Alpha and beta testing will help you provide more functional software with fewer known bugs. Use a user-reporting strategy to recreate bugs more easily in your working machine and resolve them as soon as possible. Clearing bugs requires experience and, at times, an expert opinion. Don't be afraid to ask for help in forums.

Keep a healthy work-life balance

Regardless of your chosen profession, keeping a balance between work and personal life is important. To get the most out of your work time, especially as a programmer, you must be aware of tasks and time management. If you work as a freelancer, apps like Things and Session can help you manage your tasks effectively. Furthermore, using techniques like the Pomodoro technique can help you clear more bugs in less time.

What Next?

I'm glad you're along for the ride as we learn Python. Programming is enjoyable, and no matter how fast you learn, only practice will make you a great developer. So, using the knowledge you've gained from this book, start working on your projects.

If you're stumped as to what projects to try, here are some project ideas to get you started.

- Create a management system for a public library in your community.

- Create a suburban metro railway reservation system.

- Using the Django library, create a simple website.

- Use Pygame to create a classic Python game.

- Parse Twitter data to build a bot that automatically retweets popular tweets.

I hope that your personal growth journey is successful in every way!

Acknowledgments

Writing a technical book is never an easy task. It requires a lot of time, effort, and focus. This book is no exception. The journey of writing this book has been full of challenges and struggles, but I am grateful for the experience.

I would like to express my deep gratitude to one of my professors, Mr. Albert Johnson. He has been a constant source of inspiration and guidance throughout my academic and professional life. His teachings on programming have been invaluable to me and I have tried my best to incorporate his wisdom and insights in this book.

I would also like to thank my coworker Alex very much. He's been very encouraging to me as I've worked on this project. He has shared his expertise, provided constructive feedback and encouraged me to push through the difficult moments.

I owe the greatest debt of gratitude to my wife Kate, who has always been there for me and pushed me forward. She has been my number one cheerleader and has never wavered in her faith in me, even when I questioned my own abilities. Her love, understanding and patience have sustained me through the long nights of writing and editing.

I also want to take a moment to thank you, the reader, for taking the time to delve into the world of Python and SQL with me. Your support and interest in this book is what makes all of the hard work and struggles worth it.

As you embark on your journey to become a skilled programmer, I want to encourage you to never give up. While the path to mastery may be exhausting, the benefits of succeeding are well worth the effort. Anything worth having is worth working hard for, and if you put in the time and effort, you can get it.

So, take a deep breath, embrace the challenge, and **never stop learning**. The possibilities are endless, and I have no doubt that you will succeed in your endeavors.

Thank you for joining me on this journey, and I hope you enjoy the book.

Philip

References

Parmar, N. (n.d.). Conditional statement in Python. Naukri Learning. https://www.naukri.com/learning/articles/conditional-statement-in-python/

O'Neil, C. (2021, June 7). How to install Python on Windows 10. DigitalOcean. https://www.digitalocean.com/community/tutorials/install-python-windows-10

McEwen, J. (2021, May 24). Coding: What is PyCharm? Emeritus. https://emeritus.org/blog/coding-what-is-pycharm/

O'Neil, C. (2020, December 9). The Python and operator explained. Real Python. https://realpython.com/python-and-operator/

LearnPython.org. (n.d.). Variables and types. Learn Python. https://www.learnpython.org/en/Variables_and_Types

VanderPlas, J. (2018, November 20). Understanding data types in Python. Python Data Science Handbook. https://jakevdp.github.io/PythonDataScienceHandbook/02.01-understanding-data-types.html

Wilder, R. (2015). Functions. In Writing Electronic Text: A Guide to Good Practice. https://rwet.decontextualize.com/book/functions/

Arras, L. (2021, June 2). Object-oriented programming in Python 3. Real Python. https://realpython.com/python3-object-oriented-programming/

Coe, James. "SQL Basics: Working with Databases – Dataquest." Dataquest, 1 Feb. 2021, www.dataquest.io/blog/sql-basics/.

Editor, Udemy. "Advanced SQL: Explore Details of Your SQL Commands." Udemy Blog, 23 May 2014, blog.udemy.com/advanced-sql/. Accessed 14 Mar. 2023.

Pham, Huyen. "Advanced SQL Queries via Practical Examples." Tech Mint, 11 May 2020, tech-mint.com/databases/advanced-sql-queries-examples/. Accessed 14 Mar. 2023.

Schaffer, Erin. "What Is a Relational Database? A Deep Dive." Educative: Interactive Courses for Software Developers, 11 June 2021, www.educative.io/blog/relational-database-deep-dive#advantages. Accessed 14 Mar. 2023.

Timoshina, Nataliya. "What Is SQL Database: Structure, Types, Examples." Www.alphaservesp.com, 8 Feb. 2023, www.alphaservesp.com/blog/what-is-sql-database-structure-types-examples. Accessed 14 Mar. 2023.

W3Schools. "SQL Joins." W3schools.com, 2019, www.w3schools.com/sql/sql_join.asp.

Zola, Andrew. "The 34 Best Data Management Tools." Panoply.io, Panoply, 2 Mar. 2023, blog.panoply.io/28-data-management-tools-5-ways-of-thinking-about-data-management.

Made in the USA
Monee, IL
11 April 2023

31716662R00105